TESTED WAYS
TO SUCCESSFUL
FUND
RAISING

TESTED WAYS
TO SUCCESSFUL
FUND
RAISING

GEORGE A. BRAKELEY, JR.

amacom

A Division of American Management Associations

Library of Congress Cataloging in Publication Data

Brakeley, George A
    Tested ways to successful fund raising.

    Includes index.
    1. Fund raising. I. Title.
HV41.B654   361.7   79-54828
ISBN 0-8144-5531-X

Second Printing

Dedicated to the great men of my professional past:
John Price Jones, G. A. Brakeley, Sr., Bob Duncan,
Si Seymour, and Dave Church, who,
separately and together, furthered the process
of making fund raising a profession.

Preface

The dictionary defines philanthropy as "the love of mankind, especially as manifested in deeds of practical beneficence." In that case, every one of us is a philanthropist, and has benefitted from philanthropy, at one point or another in our lives. But philanthropy is—and in this country has been since Colonial times—also a vital, if often overlooked, force in our lives. For it is primarily philanthropy which fueled—to the tune of nearly $48 billion in 1980—the nation's "third sector" of numerous not-for-profit institutions, which surely play as important a part in our lives as the other two sectors, business and government. The late John D. Rockefeller III noted that

> [this third sector is] omnipresent throughout our society, yet so taken for granted that it is barely recognizable as an important social force. Millions of Americans participate in third-sector activities, contributing time or financial support, or both. The sector includes thousands of institutions indispensable to community life: churches, hospitals, museums, libraries, colleges, theater groups, symphony orchestras, and social-service organizations of all kinds.

Recognition of the value and validity of this third sector has, of course, long been given by government. Federal laws, and the laws of the various states, grant bona fide not-for-profit eleemosynary institutions privileged tax-exempt status; permit those who support them to derive significant tax benefits from their contributions; and, of course, through various gifts and grants, actually help underwrite, in part, many of their activities. Indeed, government largesse with respect to the third sector increasingly is becoming a source of serious concern, as not-for-profit organizations seek new ways of retaining and increasing public support while maintaining the independence and autonomy which are a major part of their *raison d'être.*

What all these institutions have in common is their "not-for-profit" status—*and their need to raise money.* The nearly $48 billion that Americans gave in 1980 to these organizations represented a level of generosity unique in the world, and did not happen by chance, or spontaneously, as the result of "the love of mankind." Private educational, health, religious, cultural, and civic and social welfare organizations consciously and actively *seek* this support. The term "fund raising" today refers to a sizable and sophisticated business, in which professional practitioners have developed and refined the techniques that are largely responsible for ever-increasing levels of giving by individuals, foundations, corporations, government, and other organizations. Nor can volunteerism in the form of donated time, skill, and energy on the part of millions of Americans be overlooked. Conservative estimates put the dollar worth of these volunteer efforts at approximately the same level as actual dollar contributions, yielding a total philanthropic "pie" approaching $100 billion annually.

This pie, of course, must be divided up. Today, there are approximately 500,000 registered 501(c)(3) not-for-profit organizations serving various aspects of the public weal and eligible to receive financial support for which the donors may take an income tax deduction. Experience shows that the division of funds consistently has borne a very close relationship to the skill, energy, and expertise with which a given institution tells the story of its case for support, and presents that story to a carefully identified constituency. Doing this well is an arduous undertaking that requires attention from the institution's top board and administrative leadership, as well as professionalism at the staff level. But the consistent application of basic, time-proven techniques can result, over the years, in very significant levels of philanthropic support to the institutions which take sufficient time and trouble to ensure that they receive their share of philanthropy's gift billions.

As its title indicates, this book purports to describe the methods and techniques by which not-for-profit institutions can raise money. It should be emphasized here that successful fund raising depends on the steady application of various techniques in such diverse areas as annual giving, deferred giving, capital giving, and so forth, *in the context of a carefully planned long-term approach to the institution's philanthropic needs and likely sources of support.* In other words, professional fund raising is not a "one shot" proposition; it is, or should be, a central and continuous element of every not-for-profit organization's management and operation.

Yet each institution's situation and needs are unique. Within the third sector there are almost as many different kinds, sizes, and types of institutions as there are in the business sector. This book attempts, therefore, to cover the basic information, techniques, and skills that have well-proven potential for successful application to virtually every not-for-profit eleemosynary organization in the country. It is believed that this information will be of use to the individuals who lead and manage these institutions and to those directly concerned, both within the institution and among the ranks of "outside" professional counsel, with the institutions' fund-raising and development operations. While not a step-by-step "instruction" manual, this volume is intended as a guide for the experienced "pro" and the relative newcomer and as a reference source for all concerned with philanthropy and fund raising in America today.

And today as perhaps at no time in the past, the continued strength of our private, not-for-profit educational, health, religious, cultural, and civic institutions is of supreme importance. Historically, we know that they and our democratic free-enterprise system rose and flourished together. Because they are indispensable to one another, it is not fanciful to suggest that they must stand—or fall—together.

New Englander Bob Duncan, one of the deans of this business of ours and a contemporary of the greats of yesteryear such as John Price Jones, Arnaud Marts, Carlton Ketchum, Si Seymour, and perhaps my own father, always had a pithy comment at the end of any discussion, like "What does this sugar off to?" Having trained under and worked with a number of these men, having served as a reader for McGraw-Hill in 1966 on Si Seymour's fine book, *Design for Fund-Raising*, I often enjoy a retrospective look at what this business has meant to me.

Primarily I think of it in two respects: first, the constructive, usually necessary contributions it has made to a better way of life in the United States and Canada, coast to coast, in good measure through the advice my associates and I have given to our clients; second, the fine friendships it has resulted in with our nation's business and community leaders with whom I have done business, at the volunteer level and within the profession itself. Many have become personal friends.

Blair Gordon, then chairman of Dominion Textile, a director of numerous top Canadian companies (and important enough to be attacked by the Communist party in one of its publications on who "runs" Canada), chaired the first capital campaign I ever ran, for McGill University, in 1948. Blair and his wife are Godparents to two of my daughters; he and I fished together for over 25 years—each summer's trip to Bonaventure River for Atlantic salmon was a highlight of my year, and I believe of his.

Then there was the Hon. Hartland Molson, who chaired the last capital campaign I ran for the Joint Hospital Fund (three of McGill's teaching hospitals) in 1950. I remember an almost constant stream of fine weekends and great social occasions. Others include Laurance Rockefeller and Harold Helm, in New York; Louis Sudler in Chicago; Edgar Queeny in St. Louis; Jimmy Carmichael and John Sibley in Atlanta; Parmer Fuller in San Francisco; Fritz Ingram in New Orleans; Bishop John Walker and Huntington Harris in Washington; and Leonard Firestone, Justin Dart, and Tom Nickell in Los Angeles.

I would go on and on with the names of friends and acquaintances encountered through clients with whom I've been rather personally involved, including the Los Angeles County Art Museum, Harvard University, the University of Minnesota (ten years of professional counseling there), Michigan State University, the University of Michigan, USC, Dartmouth, Purdue, Affiliated Hospitals in Boston (three of Harvard's teaching hospitals), Emory, Vanderbilt, Houston, Samaritan Health Services in Phoenix, Memorial Sloan-Kettering Cancer Center, the United States Olympic Committee, the Washington Cathedral, and, right after World War II, the New York Committee of the American Cancer Society and the Salvation Army's Annual Maintenance Appeal—and so many others.

The common denominator to these associations has been senior business officers who have provided exemplary volunteer leadership in raising what I expected must be $5 or $6 billion through the companies which I have been privileged to head from coast to coast, in both the United States and Canada.

The common denominator to these associations has been senior business officers who have provided exemplary volunteer leadership in raising what I expect must be $9 or $10 billion through the companies which I have been privileged to head from coast to coast, in both the United States and Canada.

One of the fundamental propositions of the Reagan administration is that America must adhere more closely to the principles of the free-enterprise system, in which government's role will be diminished, and that of the private and business sectors will be enlarged. Dire indeed has been the weeping, wailing, and gnashing of teeth of a host of interest groups which anticipate the goring of their favorite ox. Special and legitimate concern has been voiced by educational, health, cultural, and civic and social welfare organizations which have traditionally depended on philanthropic support, and in more recent years, have come to rely on government funding as well. "What will become of us and those we serve?" is a question these organizations are asking.

Although this problem has prompted many complicated answers, my own response is a simple one. First, it is plain that these eleemosynary institutions must work harder than ever to gain a greater share of the "uninvited billions" which I discuss in Chapter 1. Second, it is my conviction that the current economic and political climate holds enormous *promise* for nonprofit institutions, provided they go about seeking those uninvited billions aggressively and imaginatively. As shown by the last election, millions of Americans, and the American business community as a whole, once again want to take more direct and more active responsibility for the nurturing and sustenance of the nation's essential private, nonprofit educational, health, cultural, civic and social welfare organizations.

To reestablish a true *quid pro quo* relationship, private philanthropy—individual and corporate—must assume a greater proportion of the eleemosynary institutions' needs. This is a small price to pay to guarantee their independence from excessive government control and regulation. Thus the "third sector" has an unparalleled opportunity, *if* these institutions proceed confidently, promptly, and professionally, to plan and implement imaginative and assertive new fund-raising strategies, policies, and programs. It is my conviction that as a group they have the ability to do this. I am convinced that they also have the will.

In closing, I like to think that I've done more than my share in the interests of our company's clients, particularly those I've served personally, and the business of philanthropy *in toto*. As I look back on the billions we have helped raise, and the fine things these monies have accomplished, I view them more in terms of the people I've known and enjoyed than the bricks-and-mortar, and the dollars, involved. It's a people business I'm in, and it's people who've given me my greatest rewards.

Acknowledgments

The author gratefully acknowledges the help received in writing this book from John J. Schwartz, President, American Association of Fund-Raising Counsel. In addition, the aid of my associates, including Mrs. Tina F. Daniels and Messrs. Edward Blair, John Leslie, William O'Connor, and James Steeg, was invaluable. Steven Paradis conducted much of the basic research, and served as editorial supervisor. Finally, I am indebted to the members of my support staff for their many hours of dedicated typing, retyping, and proofreading of the final manuscript.

George A. Brakeley, Jr.

Contents

1

What Fund-Raising Professionals Need to Know—an Overview

American philanthropy as we know it today was "born" only two decades after the Pilgrims landed at Plymouth Rock, when the Massachusetts Bay Colony sent three clergymen back to England to raise money for nascent Harvard College. They returned bearing £500 in contributions. Until the end of the 1700s, colonial fund raising was concentrated mainly on higher education and religion. Gradually, health, civic and social causes, and the arts entered the picture as the young nation grew and prospered.

It is interesting to note that philanthropy in pre-Revolutionary America had its roots in necessity: it was the only means of building and sustaining the service institutions each community needed. Historian Henry Steele Commager has said:

> Americans managed without energetic government for so long a time that they came to prefer voluntary public enterprise. If they wanted a college, they built one—and they kept right on doing that into the 20th century; if they needed a hospital, they raised money for it; if they lacked books, they got together and collected them . . . because *participation* is the very essence of of democracy, it is difficult to exaggerate the value of this aspect of American philanthropy.

1

Some Vital Statistics

In 1980, Americans gave over *$47 billion* to 500,000 private educational, medical, religious, cultural, civic, and social welfare institutions—over $4 billion more than they gave in 1979. When the estimated value of volunteers' time and services is added to this figure, the third sector received the staggering total of nearly 100 billion philanthropic dollars in 1980.

The philanthropic "pie" has, over the past ten years, shown a fairly consistent makeup. Taking 1980, the most recent year for which figures are available, with total philanthropic giving of $47.7 billion, religion received 46.3 percent, or $22.2 billion; health and hospitals, 13.6 percent, or $6.5 billion; education, 14 percent, or $6.7 billion; social welfare, 10 percent, or $4.7 billion; arts and humanities, 6.2 percent, or $2.9 billion; civic and public organizations, 2.9 percent, or $1.4 billion; and the catchall category of "other" institutions, 7.0 percent, or $3.37 billion.

It seems likely that over the coming decade these proportions will continue to hold, with relatively minor variations, as they did in the preceding ten years, although of course no such prediction can be made with absolute certainty. Indeed, an important part of the professional fund raiser's work is to keep abreast of developments and trends in philanthropy, the economy, and society at large, particularly as they affect the institutions he is most directly concerned with. Thus the fund-raising professional concentrating primarily on higher education will foresee, and attempt to quantify, the effects of the tail-off in student enrollments forecast for the early 1980s, to take but one example. In health and medicine, the impact of a national health insurance plan and the growth of proprietary hospitals are just two of the many imponderables the fund-raising professional active in these areas must consider. Similar examples exist in religion, the arts, and civic and social causes.

The sources of the $47.7 billion philanthropic "pie" for 1980 were individual donors, who contributed $39.9 billion, or 83.7 percent of the total; gifts by bequest totaling $2.9 billion, or 6.0 percent; foundations, which gave $2.4 billion, or 5.0 percent; and corporate contributions, totaling $2.6 billion, or 5.3 percent. Again, with minor variations, this donor breakdown has held steady over the past decade and can reasonably, although not necessarily in every instance, be expected to remain fairly constant over the coming ten years.

Volunteer efforts, as noted earlier, constitute an important part of the story of American philanthropy. Although much more difficult to quantify than dollar gifts and grants, the very number of volunteers who worked on behalf of the nation's top 20 charitable organizations (as ranked by number of volunteers and excluding religious and church groups and, of course, thousands of other health, educational, arts, civic, and social welfare organizations) is perhaps astounding. Statistically 20,585,968 men and women—roughly one out of every ten Americans—served as volunteers for these 20 service organizations alone, and of this total 16,060,387 were fund-raising volunteers.

Philanthropy's Potential

Unlike many areas of human endeavor with inbuilt limitations on growth, philanthropy appears to have no *inherent* restrictions, other than those implied by the tax laws. (It is true, of course, that since giving is made possible by private earnings and wealth, it is also dependent upon them.) Impressive as the foregoing giving figures may be, it is the writer's conviction that they could be *doubled*—if the private, not-for-profit institutions which rely on philanthropy go about their development and fund-raising activities in an assertive, well-planned, professional fashion. And indeed these organizations must set some such goal if they are to continue to receive the philanthropic support they will require to sustain their present levels of operation in an inflationary period marked by steadily rising costs—characteristics which most analysts are convinced will be status quo for the remainder of the century.

Another challenge to philanthropy lies in the fact that while total giving has risen steadily, it has lagged behind the 11 percent annual growth rate which the Commission on Private Philanthropy and Public Needs concluded in 1975 charities must achieve if they are to maintain present levels of operation. The "uninvited billions" needed to close this gap unquestionably exist—but they must be pinpointed more precisely and, once sighted, sought more energetically.

The source of giving which probably has the greatest immediate potential provides an illuminating illustration of this basic point. Annually over the past decade (with the exception of only one or two years), giving by the corporate sector has grown steadily, if slowly, and has remained in fourth place, after individual gifts, bequests, and foundation support. But corporate giving as a percentage of corporate income has not kept pace with corporate growth, just as individual giving has not kept pace with increases in individual income. Over the past ten years, before-tax corporate contributions to philanthropy have *averaged* one percent annually, while federal law allows 5 percent of before-tax corporate income to be given to nonprofit charitable institutions. (There is of course no such limit on individual giving.)

The difference between what might be called a jog-trot approach to philanthropy by a community's eleemosynary institutions and business sector and an energetic, forward-pushing effort to garner the philanthropic support which charitable institutions must have is well illustrated by one presently atypical American community. Twenty-three Minneapolis firms donated *5 percent or more* of pretax earnings to civic and charitable causes in 1975. One contributor—the Northwestern National Bank—not only gave more than 5 percent but also reported that 230 officers of the bank had given more than 29,000 hours of volunteer service to 246 different church and civic organizations. The unique blend of selflessness, volunteerism, community pride, individual initiative, and professional fund-raising expertise which made this accomplishment possible tellingly illustrates the enormous potential for growth in corporate philanthropy. It is reasonable to believe that similar potential exists in the individual, bequest, and, to a perhaps lesser extent, foundation categories.

Another, somewhat different, proof of philanthropy's potential is its "track record" and "staying power." The evidence of the track record is abundantly before our eyes in the form of a half-million private educational, health, religious, cultural, civic, social welfare, and other organizations, among them many of the most prominent and prestigious institutions of their kind in the nation, and in the world. The staying power of philanthropy, in contemporary times at least, is revealed by the Philanthropic Index originated by the author (see Figure 1).

The Philanthropic Index is an indicator that reflects general

FIGURE 1. The Philanthropic Index.

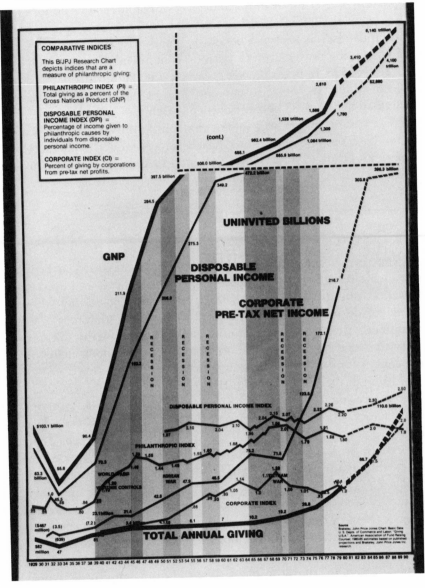

economic conditions and fluctuations in the economy and, more important, the state of mind and level of confidence of donors in all categories. It is observable that the Philanthropic Index, like other indexes, has shown a generally steady rise and very considerable staying power even in periods of financial distress, such as the 1929–1938 Depression years, when the Philanthropic Index did not follow the near 50 percent drop of the GNP but instead remained at about 83 percent of its pre-Depression level. Such examples would appear to confirm that philanthropy, although affected by economic conditions, has become so much a part of the American ethos that, at worst, it tends to plateau in bad times, and in good times, to continue upward.

The Role of the Professional

The term "fund-raising professional" is necessarily a broad one. It includes the administrators, board members, and even experienced institutional administrative and staff personnel whose principal duties are focused on fund raising (the directors of development, deferred giving, annual giving, and so forth); and professional fund-raising counsel, comprising fund-raising firms, independent fund raisers, and consultants.

Although they are not often thought of in this light, the chancellors, presidents, executive directors, and other top administrative leaders, whose broad responsibility for their institution's performance and continued fiscal health inevitably involves them directly in its development and fund-raising needs, are among the most important and best qualified fund-raising professionals today. The members of the boards of trustees and other high-level volunteer leaders at these institutions, too, are confronted frequently with the need to become actively involved in the institution's fund-raising and development planning and programs.

These men and women are seconded in this particular area of responsibility by the administrative and staff employees whose work is concerned primarily or solely with fund raising, and by professional fund-raising counsel, including firms and individuals, typically working on a fee basis. Some professionals specialize in a particular field, such as health, education, or religion;

others are acquainted with, and prepared to serve, most or all kinds of not-for-profit institutions.

In addition to a common interest in philanthropy, fund raising, and institutional development, the men and women referred to above as administrative and/or staff fund-raising professionals, and those serving as professional counsel, share other characteristics. Typically, they are college graduates with experience in both the business and not-for-profit sectors (and often government as well); they have a mastery of English which enables them to communicate effectively and persuasively, in writing and speech; they possess leadership qualities; and, perhaps as important as anything else, they are highly motivated. It is likely that few people embark on careers in fund raising in the expectation of earning a great deal of money. Rather, idealism—the belief in a particular cause or causes which are part of a larger cause and a larger purpose—is a primary motivation for the majority of men and women attracted to and working in the fund-raising profession today.

Which Fund Raisers Do What?

The top administration and the board of trustees serve as leaders and planners for all aspects of the institution's life, including fund raising and development. Their work is implemented, in most cases, by the men and women who comprise the organization's development staff. The success of an institution's development planning and fund-raising efforts almost always relates directly to how closely and effectively top administrative board-level leadership works with and communicates with the development staff and, of course, to the ability, experience, and efficiency of the development staff itself.

WITHIN THE INSTITUTION: THE DEVELOPMENT OFFICE

The Development Office, or Office of Development, is the most common name for the office in which a not-for-profit institution concentrates responsibility for the greater part of the planning, guidance, administration, and implementation of its activities that bear on the expansion of its financial resources. Usually operating under an administrator with the title of Director of Development or Vice President for Development, the Development Office seeks to identify and mobilize all that institution's resources in order optimally to define or state its case for support; to identify likely sources of support, both individuals and organizations, and to present the institution's case for support to these individuals and organizations. (The term support is being used here to denote both volunteer leadership and financial contributions.) Ideally, this is done in a carefully planned sequence within overall schedules tailored to specific development needs and objectives.

If this sounds like a large order for the Development Office and officer(s), it *is*—a very large order. A successful institutional development officer must be an excellent administrator, able to manage and supervise a staff that may number from one or two to as many as 100 people. He or she must be able to plan, to lead, to motivate staff and volunteers; to work effectively with top administration and the board of trustees; to relate well to faculty, medical staff, alumni, and other in-house "constituencies"; to establish and maintain a wide range of contacts within the local community, including the business community; and frequently to establish relationships with peers at other nonprofit institutions.

Obviously, development officers must understand well the services and purposes their organizations provide or seek to meet. They must be able to talk knowledgeably, and often in technical language, with donors, prospective donors, and others about the entire institutional "case," specific institutional needs, and the needs and plans of the community at large, including the activities of other institutions which may be seen variously as complementing and/or competing with the organization. A solid understanding of the value and uses of public relations, preferably backed by practical experience, is essential to the effective fund-raising professional.

An accomplished development officer is therefore also usually a "people" person. He or she likes people and is able to establish rapport and confidence readily with individuals of various professions, interests, and backgrounds. A successful development officer must "communicate" well in the widest sense of the word—by means of personal style and presence, which includes appearance; by manner of speech; and by ability to write. Finally, a successful development officer must be a person of the highest personal integrity and probity in all areas of business and personal life, and must know, or quickly learn, which tasks to delegate, when, and to whom.

It is safe to say that today there are far fewer such individuals seeking jobs than there are institutions in need of such men and women, although there is a growing influx in the profession of people with strong potential of all ages and from many backgrounds. While it goes without saying that not all institutional fund-raising professionals currently measure up to the highest standards, it is encouraging to note that an awareness of the need for continuing self-education and development seems to be growing—no doubt largely the result of the examples of exceptional professional achievement now more widely available for the individual to measure himself or herself against and emulate.

There are presently many thousands of men and women working as development officers and associate or assistant development officers in the nation's not-for-profit institutions. They have their own professional organizations, such as the National Society of Fund Raising Executives (NSFRE) and National Association for Hospital Development (NAHD), as well as such special societies as higher education's Council for Advancement and Support of Education (CASE).

OUTSIDE THE INSTITUTION: PROFESSIONAL FUND-RAISING COUNSEL

Professional fund-raising counsel is provided by firms and independent fund-raising consultants. In most cases, counsel is used to supplement in-house capabilities for specific facets or phases of development planning, designing and managing capital campaigns, and providing specialized consulting and services in such areas as deferred giving, annual giving, public relations and communications, direct mail, government funding, and use of the computer.

Professional counsel enables institutions to draw on a breadth and depth of experience and the resources of various individuals or an entire company, to the extent these are needed to supplement, complement, and strengthen in-house efforts or substitute for in-house staff in their absence. Professional fund-raising counsel provides a cost-effective means of obtaining important planning, research, and managerial services which very few of even the largest not-for-profit institutions could afford, or would need, to maintain on a permanent basis.

Most professional fund-raising firms subscribe to the strict code of professional ethics promulgated and regulated by the American Association of Fund-Raising Counsel (AAFRC), which was founded in 1935. Such organizations work only on a fixed-fee basis. They do not profit, directly or indirectly, from the funds the institutions they serve raise. They maintain strict confidentiality regarding all information obtained for and included in the studies they conduct, as well as information relating to gifts with confidential implications. A budget for every assignment is prepared in advance, and fund-raising firms or their clients maintain rigid budget control. Their contractual agreements routinely carry a cancellation clause applicable to both the client institution and the firm. AAFRC member firms, and most other professional fund-raising companies and individuals, will serve only those philanthropic institutions and causes whose purposes and methods of operation they approve of. They will not knowingly be used by any organization to induce individuals or organizations to support unworthy causes.

As can be seen, the basic qualifications for a successful career in fund raising are similar, and at many points overlap, for professionals working within an institution and for individuals working outside as professional counsel. It is common to find that successful fund-raising practitioners have had experience in both situations, giving them a valuable understanding of the special requirements and opportunities of both these faces of their profession and enabling them to work effectively together.

New Directions in Philanthropy

Recent years have seen the emergence or intensification of several trends in philanthropy, most notably in deferred giving, government grantsmanship (and government's role as philanthropist), direct mail, public relations and communications, and the use of the computer in data processing applications. Each of these important topics is the subject of a separate chapter.

Problems Facing Philanthropy

As with law and medicine, one of the most insistent problems facing philanthropy—and hence the fund-raising profession—is the steady encroachment of government on the activities, including the funding processes, of the nation's private, not-for profit institutions. To some extent, this encroachment reflects the reasonable consideration that as our private educational, health, cultural, civic, and social welfare institutions become more dependent upon public support, government has not only a right but an obligation to ensure that tax dollars so earmarked are utilized effectively. The danger is that the institutions' autonomy and control of planning, programs, and purposes may be eroded, thus weakening their freedom and independence—which are the major part of their *raison d'être* as private organizations. (An interesting reversal of this dilemma is the situation of *public* institutions, mainly state colleges and universities, seeking private philanthropic support to supplement their largely tax-financed budgets.)

The implications for academic freedom, for initiative in medical research, for imaginative and compassionate responses to social needs, for new directions in the arts, are serious. Historically, private institutions have thrived because of their freedom to select and focus upon specific purposes, in direct response to community and/or wider needs, without the expectation that they should be all things to all people. Yet it must be admitted even by a critic of present trends that the picture is by no means so bleak as some doom-sayers have suggested. And there may be benefits from the increased exposure and heightened examination which the issue of private versus public control of private institutions appears to be on the point of receiving, for the questions raised all appear forcefully to emphasize one basic fact: that only by maintaining and increasing their levels of private philanthropic support can the nation's not-for-profit institutions retain the independence and freedom which are essential if they are to continue to fulfill the high expectations and trust of the American people.

Because the funding of these institutions is perceived as a matter of public concern, their fund-raising activities have also come under closer scrutiny in recent times. Again, given their status as tax-exempt institutions qualified to receive tax-exempt gift dollars, this seems appropriate and even necessary. Despite arguable objections to government controls in a free-enterprise society, the threat of regulation has resulted in the nation's not-for-profit institutions setting, on the whole, an estimable fund-raising cost-effectiveness record and establishing high standards of integrity.

What controls have been imposed to date appear largely to reflect a lack of understanding of fund-raising needs and requirements—a lack the profession, and the institutions it serves, must find ways to remedy. For example, many states limit the amount that can be spent on fund-raising activities to 15 percent of total funds raised. Although reasonable, this can create problems in the relatively cost-intensive start-up phrase of a capital campaign, which may run for two, three, or even five or more years. Similarly, there are situations in which bona fide, needed, new eleemosynary institutions simply cannot get started at all if their initial investment in fund raising and development is limited to 15 percent.

Finally, it should be noted that as a rule, regulatory measures have been established, or called for, not to prevent widespread abuses, but in response to isolated, although sometimes flagrant and frequently widely publicized, instances of impropriety. Examples include cases where institutions have spent nearly as much as or even more than the amounts they raised; instances when an institution's need for and/or use of the funds it raised was challenged and found improper; and, sad to note, cases where fund-raising counsel worked on a "percentage" basis, like a debt collection agency. Such aberrant abuses attract much more public attention, of course, than is received by the great majority of private institutions and professional fund-raising firms working ably, responsibly, and conscientiously to ensure the annual recurrence of one of democracy's most remarkable phenomena: the giving of nearly $48 billion by individuals, foundations, corporations, government, and others to the not-for-profit institutions which are a key element in meeting many of the needs Americans count as among the most important in their lives.

2

The Fundamentals

Fund raising in America today is marked by three important trends: larger goals than ever before are being established almost routinely, longer campaign periods are becoming more common, and "leadership" gifts increasingly account for a larger portion of total campaign goals. While an institution's fund-raising efforts are still typically divided into such categories as capital campaigns, annual giving, and deferred giving, today the need for a long-term approach to institutional development is becoming increasingly apparent—not only for large institutions, but for medium-size and small organizations as well. The older "crisis to crisis" approach to fund raising, which worked well for some institutions and not very well for others, is simply no longer adequate for any. Institutional development and fund raising must be viewed as a continuous, ongoing responsibility, with goals set, of course, to reflect immediate and future needs.

Sound planning can result only from sound research, and research in this instance includes identifying the immediate and long-term institutional requirements and goals on the one hand and the sources of potential support for these goals on the other. (A major factor in the latter process, as we shall see, is the identification of effective leadership.) As can be seen, the two sides of the process are interdependent: an institution's development goals can be clearly defined only in terms of short- and long-term planning; leadership and financial support prospects cannot be pinpointed until this planning process has taken place and it is known just what the needs, and the case, are; and the planning itself will be dependent, to a greater or lesser degree, on the institution's analysis of its ability to attract the requisite leadership and financial support.

These facts point unmistakably in one direction: the need for accurate comprehensive analysis, supported by documented research, of the institution's goals and purposes, its importance to the constituencies it seeks to serve, and the degree to which it has interested, and can be expected to interest, potential leaders and donors.

The Case for Support

What all this boils down to is the need for every not-for-profit institution *to state its case for support*. Why does a particular college, university, medical center, symphony orchestra, religious organization, or social agency merit philanthropic support? Just what, in addition to the general benefits it can be assumed to confer, are the specific arguments for individuals, foundations, corporations, and government to single out the organization for significant financial support? Are there comparable institutions providing similar services, and if so, how is the institution in question distinguished from them? Since today there are nearly half a million 501(c)(3) institutions in America that are dependent on philanthropy to a greater or lesser degree, it can be appreciated that the institution's statement of its case for support is the primary requisite for laying the foundation of a successful fund-raising and development program.

Most not-for-profit institutions do this as a matter of course, although not always as well as they might—and today and tomorrow, must. The case for support must meet two basic criteria. First, it should be "bigger" than the institution; that is, it must relate the activities and needs of the particular college, hospital, church, or other organization to larger social endeavors and issues. Some institutions can do this more readily than others (especially for publicity purposes). An institution devoted to childhood cancer research and treatment more obviously has a case with impact carrying beyond its doors than, say, a new modern dance company. The dance company will simply have to work harder to establish its case.

The second requirement for an effective case for support is that it be related to goals which are demonstrably valid, are presented with adequate documentation of their feasibility and efficacy, are urgent, and to some extent are unique.

As a practical matter, many individuals typically will be involved in crystallizing and articulating the institution's case for support. Obviously, it must represent the thinking of the administration and board of trustees; ideally, it should also reflect long-term institutional planning that will give it validity and applicability over a number of years. The best statement per se of the case for an institution is not always produced by individuals within the institution, for the objectivity and fresh perspective of an outsider can be valuable here, if suitably employed. (This point is covered more fully in Chapters 4 and 15 in connection with the use of professional fund-raising counsel in conducting studies and "audits.") Of course, many institutions very successfully state their cases utilizing in-house talent.

Leadership

That an institution's fund-raising ability is almost always in direct proportion to the caliber and commitment of its leadership is self-evident, but it is nonetheless worth repeating. Able, dedicated leadership has been behind every private institution which has prospered and grown; those which have withered and fallen by the wayside invariably failed, for one reason or another, to attract and retain the level and kind of leadership they needed.

The board of trustees is at once the key to and the measure of an institution's leadership strength at any given moment. How able, committed, and influential in the community these individuals are will determine to a very large degree the institution's effectiveness, base of support, and "image," for the board generally both sets the tone for the administration, which in turn determines quality of staff and operations, and builds—or fails to build—a base of support. Of course, there are institutions which function well despite weak or inactive boards, and there are institutions whose boards glitter with the "best" names in the community and which yet fail to move ahead. But these are anomalies. In practically every instance, it will be found that an institution which is able consistently to attract the level of funding it needs will have a board of trustees who are true leaders in the community and who truly lead their institution.

The administration is also an important source of leadership. Top administrators of course are usually selected for this ability, among others; and it has already been noted that a successful director of development must have this quality. Within the administration there are often individuals whose specific roles do not appear, on paper, directly or sometimes even indirectly to involve them in the institution's development and fund-raising activities. Such appearances are almost always deceptive: there is virtually no administrator who should not at least be considered carefully for his or her potential to contribute to the institution's overall development efforts and to specific aspects of fund-raising programs. Too often, obvious connections are ignored by organization charts. The directors of student recruitment and of public relations and the business manager all typically have experience, information, contacts, and access to individuals or constituencies which will be found invaluable to intelligent development planning.

Nor should leadership potential at the staff level be overlooked. Obvious sources are staff members who are active in the community, who organize or participate in special institutional functions and events, and who have had experience as volunteers. Such individuals can be highly effective in organizing and promoting in-house campaigns and in helping take the institution's "story" to the larger community. Faculty members and medical staff, of course, are an excellent source of leadership for particular aspects of a campaign or development effort relating to their fields of specialty. Again, provision should be made in the thinking behind the organization charts for fully and imaginatively utilizing the abilities of the institution's staff in development efforts.

Gift Sources

Theoretically, every individual or organization affected by, benefiting from, or otherwise interested in an institution's activities and programs is a potential source of philanthropic support. Such sources need to be carefully cataloged, categorized, and translated into specific individual and organization names to be researched, cultivated, and, ultimately, solicited for support according to a realistic timetable and order of priorities. In other words, gift sources, in the broadest sense of the term, become part of the institution's "master plan" for fund raising and development.

Many institutions have found the technique known as "sequential fund raising," pioneered by Brakeley, John Price Jones Inc., to be highly effective. Sequential fund raising recognizes that the greatest part of the funds sought for a capital campaign will come from a relatively small number of donors making sizable gifts. The theory is that these prospects must be identified, cultivated, and persuaded to give before a broader-based effort can successfully be launched, and that the degree of commitment and level of giving established by their "leadership gifts" will set the pace for giving at other levels.

This approach has the merit of combining very naturally, at the outset, the need to identify leadership with the need to locate and cultivate prospects with potential for making the largest gifts. Sequential fund raising can effectively be applied to each gift category in a capital campaign, and its basic principles apply equally to the identification, cultivation, and motivation of volunteer leadership. Obviously, to succeed, sequential fund raising depends upon very accurate ranking of gift prospects according to their giving potential and likelihood of making gifts. It also depends on the institution's willingness to adhere to the sequential process throughout a campaign or other sustained development effort. In a word, it depends on *restraint*. It has the demerit, for those who find restraint distasteful, of deferring until later—until what its proponents consider the "proper time"—much of the publicity which a capital campaign or other fund-raising effort can and should generate, for in sequential fund raising upper-echelon prospects are always approached on a personal basis, by peers—a process in which they become indeed the targets of what might be called tailor-made "mini" campaigns. Given the size of gift typically sought from such individuals—ranging up to several or even many million dollars, but always in proportion to the overall campaign goal—this approach would not appear extravagant of time or effort. And consistently, over the years, for large, medium-size, and small private institutions of all kinds, results have borne out its efficacy.

There are, of course, alternative approaches to fund raising, although to date none has demonstrated the same effectiveness as the sequential approach or some variation on its basic theme. Nonetheless, quite large sums have often been raised on the basis of ad hoc solicitations, mass appeals which were not part of any larger development plan, and a variety of other schemes. In general, their weakness is that while they may succeed in producing a satisfactory level of philanthropic income at a given time, they do not build a strong base for further efforts, and by "jumping the gun" on various prospects and prospect groups, they very frequently may fail to receive the level of support that could otherwise be anticipated.

The actual sources for gifts are *individuals, corporations, foundations, clubs and other organizations, civic groups,* and *governments.* Individuals include the board of trustees, friends, administration and staff, and such other members of the institutional "family" as alumni, students, parents, and grateful patients.

Local firms and companies with which board members, administrators, and friends of the institution have close contacts are the most obvious corporate prospects, but, looking further afield, planning should also seek to match the institution's purposes and needs with known interests of various corporations and businesses in other locations. To a major extent, much corporate giving can be thought of as a *quid pro quo* proposition with the business organization often benefiting from the institution's research activities; receiving access to special laboratories to test equipment and/or processes under development; and gaining opportunities to recruit graduates.

Foundations, on the other hand, have as their specific purpose the support of various causes and institutions. Efficiency and effectiveness here are best served by first ascertaining which foundations have policies of supporting the institution's purposes, and the degree to which location and the kind of support (capital or operating) sought are factors. Also—despite the fact that grant proposals are considered dispassionately and on their own merits—it is helpful to establish leadership-level contacts with individuals connected with the foundation, whenever this is feasible.

Clubs, civic groups, and other organizations must be assessed on an individual basis. Their potential can be significant if the institution's purposes and goals fall within their support parameters, as would be likely, for example, in the case of a community neighborhood center seeking support for operating purposes from the local United Way Chapter. Today governments at the federal and state levels can be a major source of support for many private institutions, and local governments may also make various gifts and grants available. The subject of government grantsmanship as it relates to institutional development and fund raising is one of growing importance and complexity. This topic is explored in some depth in Chapter 14.

Organization

A fund-raising effort, like a military campaign, depends for success on the skill and thoroughness with which it is organized. A major investment in sound planning and organization at the outset can pay rich dividends later, not only in terms of fund-raising effectiveness per se, but also by enabling the institution to rely confidently and consistently on one scheme rather than having periodically to scramble to reorganize a poorly planned initial effort. Responsibility for planning and implementing fund-raising organization usually rests with the director of development. It is a seminal, one-time exercise which it is so important to get right that all likely sources of "input" should be considered and weighed carefully. Professional counsel may be retained to assist in the process, and probably should be retained at this juncture more often than it is. (Few corporate executives would hesitate to engage outside management consultants, whose experience and objectivity would be difficult to duplicate internally on the scale required, for a critical start-up process, and few eleemosynary institutions can afford not to get the best advice and guidance they can in organizing for fund raising.) The basic patterns of this organization, including the roles of volunteers, staff, the internal institutional "family," and professional counsel, are explored in subsequent chapters.

Public Relations

As suggested in the earlier discussion of sequential fund raising, public relations plays an important part in an institution's development efforts. Indeed, good PR and favorable publicity are essential to establishing and reinforcing the institution's basic case for support. Yet oddly, for many years there was an unwritten rule among some private institutions to the effect that they were "above" publicity, or at any rate above seeking it, and that their achievements spoke more loudly than any words in the "media." Today, such a notion brings smiles to the faces of all but the most obdurate adherents of a rapidly vanishing code of institutional aloofness. Indeed, increasingly the public relations office is "where it's at" in terms of the institution's image—an image which affects the attitudes of individual donors and potential donors of all levels; of foundation and corporation executives; of volunteers; of the press and community opinion molders; of the "customers" for the institution's services, be they students, patients, audiences, or congregations; and of state legislatures and other bodies controlling the public purse strings.

Nevertheless, it is surprising how frequently private institutions fail to put their best foot forward—indeed, too many still appear, however unintentionally, to hide their light under a bushel until some unwelcome (and usually trivial) but highly publicized development blows their "cover." It is important that an institution's board, administration, development office, and professional counsel be aware of the critical role public relations can, and in most cases must, play in successful fund raising. Just as institutional development today has become a continuous, ongoing process, so must good public relations be viewed as a constant necessity, not only to buttress the institution's development efforts, but to reinforce its efforts in all areas of operation. Professional counsel is frequently called upon to assist with long- and short-term public relations planning and management, and obviously it is essential that such counsel consider fully the impact of the institution's public relations efforts on its fund-raising plans and programs.

Budgets

It is axiomatic that an institution must spend money in order to raise money. Therefore, budgets adequate to do the job well will have to be established. The question most frequently raised is "How much money must we spend?" Of course, the answer will vary from one institution to the next according to a variety of factors such as the extent of development resources already available, the magnitude of fund-raising goals, and so on.

One general rule can be stated, however: the apparent lack of the funds needed to do the job right should never be accepted as an excuse for doing it badly. Since there is no single endeavor more crucial to an institution's future than developing adequate fund-raising capability, this need must receive the same budgetary priority as other comparable needs. Approached this way, any viable institution can, and will, find the requisite funds. Other factors to consider include such variables as the availability of in-house personnel and office resources; the need, when beginning or upgrading a development operation, to allow for the "amortization" of the initial expenditure over what should be years of heightened productivity; and recognition that, in order to remain or to become competitive for its share of philanthropic dollars, an institution must be willing to match similar or competing institutions in budgeting for fund raising. Of course, the ultimate measure is the return on the investment and the cost-effectiveness of the campaign, questions treated further on in this chapter.

Annual Campaign vs. Capital Campaign

The importance of keeping separate, and in clear focus, these two quite different kinds of philanthropic support can hardly be overstated. Many well-laid development plans have gone astray as a result of failure to make it clear to donors and prospects just how capital and annual giving interrelate—from the institution's standpoint and, just as important, from the donor's point of view.

Annual giving is the effort by an institution each year to raise a given sum of money, which usually increases annually. For many institutions, especially those lacking significant endowments, income from annual giving can literally be the organization's lifeblood. For colleges, hospitals, arts institutions, and civic and other groups, the annual appeal is often the only way the inevitable gap between expenses and income can reliably be bridged. Some institutions have gone to considerable lengths to explain this to their supporters, often using the "living endowment" illustration in which the income derived from annual giving is equated with the income a hypothetical endowment would have yielded. An annual-giving income of $500,000 could thus be said to "replace" the income from a $10 million endowment (figuring earnings at 5 percent)—if the institution had it. Obviously, any disruption in annual-giving income will affect an institution very seriously—and usually immediately. The success of annual-giving programs for thousands of private, not-for-profit institutions, including college and university alumni programs, demonstrates how effective these organizations have been in educating their constituencies as to the role annual giving plays.

The announcement of a capital campaign can cause alarming ripples on the placid surface of the most successful annual giving program. Although the implications of the term "capital campaign" may seem obvious enough to those familiar with it, they are not obvious to many donors (and, indeed, since capital campaigns often seek funds for endowment, legitimate confusion can easily arise). What must be explained clearly is that a capital campaign seeks funds for *specific capital purposes*, sometimes including endowments, and has nothing to do with the institution's annual, recurring operating deficit.* Since operating expenses will remain the same, or more likely increase, during the capital campaign, the importance of each individual maintaining his or her level of annual giving is as great as ever. The confusion of the two campaigns is no doubt often furthered by the puzzling but effective technique of crediting annual giving to the capital campaign for all or part of its duration, in an effort to keep up annual support while boosting the capital effort. The hope is that this will lead donors to give more to each, or both, than they otherwise might.

Experience shows that these difficulties can largely be avoided if clear explanations are given of precisely what the relationship is between each campaign and the institution's overall development goals, and what the institution is asking supporters to do on behalf of both. Obviously, this requires good communication and full cooperation among the various administrators and depart-

---

*Capital giving implies gifts out of the donor's capital assets, usually over a period of years, as opposed to gifts out of income.

ments concerned. A good fund-raising organization plan will provide for this by recognizing the need for fluent exchanges of information and genuine cooperation by the annual-giving-campaign administration and staff, the alumni office, the capital-campaign administration and staff, and the office of public relations.

Cost Effectiveness and Accountability

In many ways, this subject is the bottom line of institutional fund raising. Obtaining a sufficient level of philanthropic support must be done on a cost-effective basis, and strict accountability maintained, if the institution's development and fund-raising efforts are to be productive and win the degree of internal and external confidence needed for continued growth.

A standard rule of thumb for cost effectiveness (mandated by law in many states) is that total expenditures for fund-raising purposes should not exceed a certain percentage of funds raised in a given year. In instances where an institution is close to, or up to, this maximum—usually 15 percent—expansion of current efforts *must* be accompanied by contained or reduced expenditures in one or more areas of the fund-raising operation. The decision to retain professional counsel must take this requirement into account.

The problem most commonly caused by fixed cost-effectiveness requirements is that they lack the elasticity to accommodate the initial or start-up costs for a major capital campaign or other effort. Effective and successful campaigns can be, and routinely are, accommodated well within the 15 percent guideline when expenditures are averaged over the campaign's duration, which often is several years, but the high front-end costs can pose problems. Fortunately, most institutions have a sufficient degree of flexibility in their internal budgeting procedures to make it possible to accommodate this problem. In-house personnel and physical resources can be reallocated, budgets earmarked for fund raising per se spread over the projected campaign period, and funds allocated for the campaign proper used partially to cover ongoing development expenses.

One of the reasons professional fund-raising counsel is so important to many institutions is the very high cost-effectiveness benefits it typically confers, bringing to the institution—only for the length of time required—a range of practical experience and skills that would be prohibitively expensive to provide by "staffing up." Despite occasional stories of flagrant abuses, on the whole, American philanthropy has established and maintained an enviable cost-effectiveness record. The main reason for this is undoubtedly that ability to demonstrate satisfactory cost effectiveness, good accountability, and of course good stewardship in the use of the funds raised are prerequisites for all institutions seeking serious philanthropic support.

3
Donor Motivations

Human behavior is a complex and much-studied phenomenon. Numerous theories, often at variance with one another, have been evolved to explain why people behave as they do and what their actions really "mean." Certainly no review of philanthropy and fund raising would be complete without an exploration of the major identifiable reasons people give money. What actually motivated American individuals and organizations to give nearly $48 billion in 1980 to the nation's not-for-profit organizations and philanthropic causes?

This chapter will approach the topic from a subjective, pragmatic standpoint, based on some forty years of professional experience. The reader will note that the identifiable factors which clearly motivate giving sometimes correspond to various currently popular psychological, social, and economic explanations for certain aspects of human behavior; that altruism is one of many possible motives—but usually the chief one; and that, in most individual cases, careful analysis will reveal several interrelated factors at work.

The Nine Key Factors

Practically every fund-raising campaign or other development program depends, to a greater or lesser degree, on one or more of the following factors in motivating donors to support the institution.

1. Individuals, corporations, and foundations have money to give.
2. The right person or persons ask them, at the right time, and in the right circumstances.
3. People have a sincere desire to help other people.
4. People wish to belong to or be identified with a group or organization they admire.
5. Recognition of how vital their gifts can be satisfies a need for a sense of personal power in many people.
6. People have received benefits—often, personal enjoyment, as from a symphony orchestra—from the services of the organization and wish, in turn, to support it.
7. People give because they "get something" out of giving.
8. People receive income and estate tax benefits from giving.
9. People may *need* to give; that is, altruism may not be an option but a "love or perish" necessity for many people.

A cynic might consider the seventh reason people give to be the most influential one, and it may well be. Certainly a corporation normally expects some kind of *quid pro quo* return on its philanthropic "investments"—often in the form of enhanced "image," or, at a university, for example, a better welcome for its corporate recruiting program and, generally, simple recognition for services rendered. Special interest groups naturally tend to consider how a gift to a cause will advance their own efforts. Government officials will ask themselves how well a specific grant will fulfill the requirements of the law mandating it. Individuals, among a host of other possible reasons, often want either the recognition or satisfaction (or both) which comes from support of a worthy cause.

The obvious point is that most positive human behavior is motivated to some degree by enlightened self-interest, and the human need to "get something out of giving" should be steadily borne in mind by the fund-raising professional. Let us now look at some of the chief factors which motivate philanthropy and see how they apply to fund raising.

Acceptance. People generally want to belong to worthwhile groups or causes. By giving to a particular philanthropic cause, they often gain acceptance from those already involved. A fund-raising application of the need for acceptance is often observed in the sequential fund-raising process. For example, in a large, multimillion-dollar campaign, a group of 125 individuals might provide 85 percent of the campaign goal. Clearly, this "inner" group would comprise individuals of wealth, power, and influence in the community. In addition to a desire to support the cause per se, some individuals may be motivated to give because they wish to associate themselves more closely with the other members of this group.

Altruism. Altruism and humanitarianism are strong motivating forces. The desire to help an organization performing work beneficial to others, a wish to improve mankind, a sense of responsibility to the next generation are, happily, widespread. The most direct application of this observation in fund raising is probably to take special pains, when preparing case statements and other materials and organizing a campaign's public relations efforts, to present the institution or cause, and the reason it merits support, as clearly and persuasively as possible. An obvious requirement—but one which frequently is not fully met.

Appreciation. This term has application here in two senses: first, the gratitude and respect which accrue to a donor from the recipient organization, the community at large, his friends and acquaintances, and second, the expression of the donor's appreciation of the institution which his gift signifies. An important way of relating appreciation, in the first sense, to fund raising is to provide opportunities for acknowledgment of a gift. These include publication of the donor's name in an honor roll, personal thanks by the president of the institution and/or the campaign chairman, recognition at a special event, presentation of a suitable honor or award, and providing for the donor's name (or the name of some other person he wishes to honor) to be permanently memorialized by the institution on a building, an endowed chair, or a scholarship fund.

Approval. Related to appreciation, approval in the sense employed here connotes a stronger emotion, often related to self-aggrandizement. The donor making the largest gift may be demonstrating that he has "arrived"; the son out-giving his father may have a particular need to assert his strength in this way, which is not directly connected with his other reasons for giving; the individual who "names" an institution or building may be seeking to consolidate the family's social position. These examples might best be viewed as the "other side" of the picture in terms of donor motivation—for few people give *solely* for such reasons. The applicability of these observations to fund raising is to underscore the need to acquire as much knowledge about each major-gift prospect, and his or her interests, as possible. (The important subject of prospect research is treated in Chapter 5.)

Being asked. This is one of the most important motivating forces in fund raising—people simply like to be asked. They must, of course, be asked in the right way, at the right time, and for the right amount. Many individuals and organizations do not give to their full capacity, because they are asked for less than they are capable of giving or not approached or "cultivated" effectively. The subject of gift solicitation is treated in Chapter 5.

Belief in the cause (or intimate knowledge of the cause). This factor is a primary one in motivating giving. A clear exposition of the case for the institution or cause is obviously essential. Often but not always, the perceived degree of importance or urgency of the cause to some degree determines people's predisposition to "believe" in it. Cancer research, or a children's hospital, are likely to have more appeal in this sense than a library or a theater company. Once again, the importance of knowing enough about key-gift prospects to intelligently match them to specific approaches and opportunities is paramount. It is usually, though not invariably, unproductive to seek significant support from an individual or organization known to have a strong interest in higher education, say, for a social welfare agency. And, of course, it is axiomatic that an institution or a cause which is unable to generate a reasonable degree of conviction among prospects is unlikely to be able to raise significant amounts of money.

Community support. Frequently, the corporate or community leader who heads a philanthropic cause is motivated by the desire for recognition and support from the community. This wish frequently is particularly strong among business leaders, and their interest in assuming leadership roles in fund-raising programs for the community's eleemosynary institutions should always be taken into account. (See Chapter 5 on leadership identification and recruitment.)

Competition. Competition can be a major motivating factor for both leadership and giving. The "need to win" component of many individuals' personalities, and its importance to their business success, can be used productively in fund raising. Similarly, the competitive spirit, productively channeled, can be a significant element in the success of a capital campaign or other development effort.

Gratitude. This is a powerful, unselfish motive for giving which often plays a major role in an institution's fund-raising programs. The student who received a scholarship, the patient whose life was saved by a critical operation, the opera lover grateful for a lifetime of enriching performances are representative of individuals whose gratitude can be an important factor in giving, or increasing the size of a gift, to a philanthropic organization.

Group support. This motivation is based on the universal human need to belong to groups which share common interests and values. Its most common application to fund raising is a variety of forms of donor recognition. As an example, an alumnus who receives the annual honor roll of donors usually looks first for his own name, then for those of classmates who have given—particularly those he would want to have see his name on the list.

Guilt feelings. There are people who give from a sense of guilt or in order to right a wrong they feel in some way responsible for. Some donors are motivated to give from a feeling of guilt about not doing more for mankind; an alumnus who committed an expensive prank or serious infraction might seek to atone for it by giving generously to the institution. The actual applicability to fund raising of this donor motivation is obviously somewhat limited but should be borne in mind in approaching individuals who are known to be concerned about what they can do to improve the lot of mankind or to right social injustices.

Immortality. The desire for "immortality" or permanent remembrance of a loved one can be a strong motivating factor for large gifts. Individuals known to have such wishes should be offered appropriate opportunities in the form of personal proposals to permanently name an institution, a building, a program, or an endowed chair or scholarship.

"Leave me alone." There are individuals, including many who are extremely wealthy, who wish to be left alone. Sometimes such people are motivated by an opportunity to make one large gift,

pledged over many years, on the theory—or sometimes the specific stipulation—that the institution will henceforth "keep off their back," giving them immunity from further solicitation.

Playing God. Sometimes a prospective donor will seek to prove his or her power by "playing God" and refusing to give. This motivation can often be turned around by means of a special presentation designed to take into account the prospect's desire for power (or retaining total control) and offering an opportunity to fund something he or she is known to favor and which only his or her money can make possible.

Power and influence. It is well known that many successful individuals thrive on the daily challenge of "running" organizations and people and getting the job done. Such individuals should be identified for the valuable roles they can play in campaign leadership.

Preventive giving. This motivation has particular application to health organizations. The basic rationale is something like, "Help find a cure for cancer now (so if you get cancer we'll be able to cure you)." Of course, application has to be made sensitively and appropriately. Circumstances often heighten the peculiar urgency of this motivation. An example is the hospital director who died of cancer in the middle of a major capital campaign. His death had a dramatic effect on giving by a few large donors.

Return on investment (and tax benefits). Donors are naturally most strongly motivated to give to those institutions which look as if they are "going somewhere" or, in business terms, are likely to yield a good return on investment. The return, of course, can take many forms—and virtually every worthwhile eleemosynary institution should be able to demonstrate the value and benefit of continuing, expanding, or strengthening its programs. Philanthropic giving can also result in substantial tax benefits, which can significantly affect giving decisions. Fund raisers should, of course, take pains to point out the ways in which an "investment" in a given institution is likely to pay off, and the specific tax benefits which can accrue to the donor. (The latter subject is often treated in special campaign publications concerned with the ways of making gifts, and their tax implications.)

Salvation. Whether driven by guilt feelings or seeking insurance for the time when they "go to their reward," there are individuals who have a hope they may be put in better standing with the Almighty because of their benefactions. Religious institutions are, of course, the most obvious potential beneficiaries of this motivation, but when related to altruism, it can also have valid applicability to a variety of organizations and causes.

Sympathy. The term is used here to describe a strong emotional wish to help others in need or distress—a sense of caring, in other words, allied to powers of empathy. The individual who worked his way through college may more readily sympathize with the needs of scholarship students today; the parent with healthy children can hardly help being touched by the poster of the crippled child.

For fun. This last motivation is a major, and positive, factor, in the non-frivolous sense of "fun." It might better perhaps be called the "joy of giving" which has been experienced by millions of people and embraces many of the foregoing motivations. The opportunity to see one's money doing good, the sense of camaraderie that can come from working with one's peers in a worthy cause, and the satisfaction of knowing one has acted positively for good can be intensely rewarding sensations—reflecting, it might be thought, not only the Biblical belief that it is more blessed to give than to receive, but the deep-seated psychological and emotional need present in most individuals to express their "love for mankind" through active benevolence.

To summarize, effective application of awareness of donor motivations in fund raising depends on using common sense and acquiring a true understanding of people and their individual interests, ambitions, and psychological needs. More than anything else, this underscores the importance of thorough, accurate prospect research, as described in Chapter 5. For the philanthropic volunteer, campaign chairman, development officer, professional consultant, and others involved in fund raising on a part-time or full-time basis, one of the great rewards of their work, indeed, is that the motives of those who make it possible—the donors—are in almost every case fundamentally, and in most instances fervently, directed toward the betterment of mankind and the many causes civilization continues to reckon among its most important endeavors.

4

Market Research

The term "market research" is most commonly associated with the introduction of new consumer products, and with the need accurately to determine the degree of demand for, and likely acceptance of, a given new product. The "test marketing" is usually done on a geographical basis, and, of course, people's *perceptions* of the product and its "image" as conveyed through advertising are as important to the study as their reaction to the product itself.

Some of these observations apply to market research in the sense the term will be used in this chapter—market research in fund raising. In this case, the philanthropic organization or cause, and its specific goals and needs, can be viewed as the "product," while the "market" is all the individuals and organizations which comprise its constituencies for potential support. Pursuing this analogy, the capital or other campaign replaces the advertising campaign (although, interestingly, many fund-raising efforts rely heavily on promotion of various kinds, including advertising). The major difference, of course, is that fund-raising market research is concerned with determining the availability of funds, and the willingness of those who hold them to use them, for an organization or agency whose purposes are of benefit to mankind in a larger and higher sense than, say, a new brand of razor or toothpaste.

Fund-raising market research, then, directs searching questions to very carefully defined groups of individuals and organizations which have been identified as representative of the organization's primary and most likely sources of support. The process is sometimes referred to as a "feasibility study," although this term is something of a misnomer since the purposes of professional market research to determine a not-for-profit institution's fund-raising potential extend considerably beyond the attempt to produce a simple "yea" or "nay" answer. Regardless of the specific recommendations which follow from such a study process, the institution *should* acquire a great deal of extremely valuable information—much of which could not be obtained in any other way—about itself and about the external constituencies on which it relies.

Assuming that there is good cause to consider a fund-raising program for the organization and that its overall circumstances and needs are justifiable, reasonably urgent, and can be defined in principle, market-research studies for philanthropic institutions ask—and should answer—the following key questions:

Does the case for support have validity and appeal? Does the proposed fund-raising program meet the organization's needs and the needs of those who presently or potentially will use its services? Is the institution itself strong enough to sponsor the program? Is the financial objective commensurate with the needs?

Is qualified leadership available within the institution? If not, can it be attracted from elsewhere? Who are the strongest potential leaders in its support areas? Is supporting leadership available? And, specifically, what leadership is available to take on which particular responsibilities?

How much money can be raised? The announced goal obviously depends on the answer to this important question. What are the generic sources of support, and tentative quotas for each? Under what conditions are the necessary funds obtainable? Is there a sufficient number of "big" gifts potentially available to fit into the pattern of presently successful capital-gifts programs? What specific prospects can be identified, and in what approximate amounts or gift ranges? What "pace-setting" gifts are available? What degree of support can be anticipated from the various foundations and (if applicable) governmental sources? What areas of support, if any, contain possibilities of presently unidentifiable and/or incalculable potential large gifts?

What are the organizational requirements for the proposed program? What range of fund-raising coverage is recommended, and what form, consequently, should the organization for the proposed program take? What printed materials, special presentations, fund-raising publicity, and public relations efforts will be required? What functions, responsibilities, and working relations should be assigned to which key positions and committees? What are the requirements for office management, prospect research, and list development?

What basic plan of action will be most effective? This can be defined only by answering such questions as: What is the rationale or strategy underlying the proposed pattern of campaign organization? What are the enlistment requirements? What decisions have to be made and in what order? What are the first steps to be taken?

How long will it take to raise the funds? What are the planned periods of active fund raising? What are the principal activities in each stage of the program's progressive development?

How will the program be staffed? What services can be performed by the organization's existing staff? What additional staff may be needed, and for what length(s) of time? What functions will be performed by various fund-raising and public relations personnel?

Will professional counsel be used? What can be expected of professional counsel in the institution's particular circumstances? How will counsel interface with in-house staff? What kind of management service is recommended? How can suitable counsel be found?

How much will the program cost? What are the total costs involved in underwriting the fund-raising program? What will the fees for counsel be? What other expenses must be anticipated?

The foregoing questions are meant to show the extent of the application of "market research" techniques to fund raising. (Most of the points raised in such questions are covered at greater length in various other chapters of this book, as identified in the Index.) Several of the key elements of institutional market research, as it relates to fund raising, will now be considered. The reader is referred to Chapter 2 ("The Fundamentals") and Chapter 5 ("Procedures") for amplification of many of these important points.

The Case

Practically every worthwhile philanthropic organization has a case for support. In order to raise money, however, in most instances the case must be based on demonstrable needs whose validity and, ideally, urgency can persuasively be documented. A market research study, once under way, often reveals that important elements of an institution's case may appear weak to study respondents. (Or, for that matter, the project or purpose for which the fund-raising program is intended may be perceived as unnecessary, inadequately thought out, in conflict with similar plans of other institutions, and so forth.) The point is that in light of study findings, the case, as originally stated, may need to be revised slightly or significantly.

Leadership

Assuming a sound, valid, and appealing case, the organization must determine whether it has the leadership available to translate the case into tangible support. As a rule, when an organization has a sound case and the requisite leadership, it has a good chance of obtaining the funds it seeks. Indeed, because leadership is so critical to the success of any fund-raising program, the enlistment of a general chairman and members of the top leadership team should receive the same kind of concentrated effort and personal attention as the solicitation of a million-dollar gift. The subject of leadership identification and solicitation is covered in detail in Chapter 5.

Sources of Support

Identifying potential sources of support is an important aspect of the market research study. A professional study can and should identify, through the interview process, a cross-section of the best prospects within the various gift ranges. Analysis of identified sources of support permits setting realistic quotas or "targets" for the principal soliciting categories—trustees, alumni, faculty, medical staff, corporations, foundations, and so forth.

Selection of Respondents

THE EXTERNAL AUDIENCE

Obviously, the study's value depends heavily on the quality of the respondents chosen. They should include individuals who can speak with real authority on the validity of the institution's case and development plans and on the philanthropic sources available to the organization.

Consequently, the "power structure" of the community must be carefully analyzed. The individuals with financial and social leverage, with wealth or access to wealth, and those who shape opinion and/or make it their business to keep abreast of opinion are of primary importance.

THE INTERNAL AUDIENCE

Prior to the external interviews, key organization staff will also be interviewed. The basic purpose of these interviews is to determine the extent to which the institution's advancement services are available and/or adequate to support the proposed fund-raising campaign. The information required falls into three broad areas, as indicated in the following partial listing. (Chapters 2 and 5 enlarge on many of these points.)

I. General
   (a) Planning.
   (b) Scheduling.
   (c) Prospecting (research, records, staff screening, volunteer screening, rating, assigning).
   (d) Organizing (leadership committees—trustees, nucleus, leadership, corporations, foundations, deferred gifts and bequests, alumni/patients/members, staff, major/special/general, public relations, and so on).
   (e) Soliciting and reporting (sequential fund raising, worker training, prospect cultivation, soliciting, reporting and receipting, acknowledgments, publicizing, follow-ups).
II. Administration
   (a) Campaign plans.
   (b) Organization charts.

(c) Operating schedules and timetables.

(d) Office management.

(e) Budget.

(f) Computer usages.

(g) Prospect research.

(h) Gift-control procedures and finances.

(i) Top leadership meetings.

(j) Staff meetings.

III. Public Relations

(a) Plan.

(b) Printed materials.

(c) Worker training.

(d) Audiovisuals and multimedia.

(e) Prospect cultivation.

(f) Press, radio, and TV.

(g) Special events.

The Interviewer's Roles

The interviewer is, theoretically, an objective, impartial "gatherer of the facts." His/her task is to obtain as much pertinent information as possible for subsequent analysis and use. A second and equally important requirement is that the interviewer preserve the total confidentiality of all respondents' comments. (Obviously, interview reports must be handled with great care to ensure that their confidentiality is never violated.)

Yet, in the nature of the job, the interviewer is much more than a mere passive accumulator of cold facts. Indeed, the interviewer's ability to readily establish rapport with a variety of individuals, win their confidence, and convey a sense of genuine interest and even enthusiasm about the institution under discussion is of crucial importance. The interviewer, whether staff, volunteer, or professional fund-raising counsel, is always "speaking for" the organization, at least to the extent that he/she is temporarily representing it.

The interviewer's appearance, manner, and professionalism must instill confidence in the process and the institution. The interviewer must be able to explain in appropriate language just what it is that the study seeks to accomplish, what the institution's needs are, and why they are important. Obviously, a thorough acquaintance with the proposed fund-raising program, the case, the institution itself, and, as far as possible, the local community, is essential. Useful aids in the study process include the following written materials, which should be in hand for each interview:

A one-sheet table of needs.
A one-sheet summary of the "case."
A list of the trustees.
Lists and gift records of the top individual, corporate, foundation, and other prospects (ten or so from each category).
A tentative campaign organization chart.
A tentative gift-range table.
Photographs and drawings of special capital needs.

Obviously, not all of these will be used in most interviews; many respondents will be (or should be) sufficiently familiar with the institution or cause that none of them will be necessary. (A sure indication of a weak respondents list is the discovery—which does happen occasionally—that many respondents appear to know little or nothing about the organization.) On the other hand, these materials often help respondents relate known interests, giving habits, and levels of giving ability to potential gifts to the institution, as well as enabling them to more precisely define potential leadership, strengths and weaknesses of the case, and so forth. A successful interview is one in which the respondent has crossed the natural psychological barrier that separates him from the interviewer/organization and, unwittingly, begins to look at the situation from *its* point of view. It is at this point that the most useful insights, comments, and suggestions are likely to be made. The materials listed above, of course, are simply aids to fostering this atmosphere.

For certain key interviews—the university president, the board chairman, selected trustees and institutional friends, top business, government, and social leaders—it can be productive to use the team approach, in which a senior interviewer asks most of the questions and guides the discussion while the junior takes the notes and transcribes them.

The Study Report

The study report presents the findings and conclusions of the market research process, specific recommendations, and usually a plan of action. Since the study report should serve as a campaign Bible and blueprint, conciseness, brevity, and clarity are essential. Long, involved reports are indeed often prepared. It is questionable how pertinent much of the information they contain really is to the point, and it is reasonable to assume that excessive length and detail in such a report will make it less, not more, useful and likely to be used.

The main sections of the report are discussed below.

PART I: FINDINGS AND CONCLUSIONS

This analysis should cover the case, leadership, and sources of support. There should be a discussion of both positive and negative factors reported by respondents, followed by a specific indication of the amount of money which it appears can be raised. The interviewer should be prepared to identify potential and probable "big" gifts by approximate amounts. In this way a likely gift-range table can be prepared.

PART II: RECOMMENDATIONS

This section of the report presents specific recommendations in light of the study findings and conclusions. Although it draws upon hard facts, these nevertheless must be interpreted and applied intelligently and imaginatively. For example, it is usually found in the study process that for each plus factor there is a minus factor (assuming a complete and objective interview pattern), or, at least, that factors are frequently positive and negative in a complementary way. For instance, the board of trustees may have some strong leadership, but that leadership may be mainly among older members. A recommendation thus might be that, for the future, the board be strengthened in the appropriate areas. Or it may be found that qualified leadership is available, but there is some question as to whether it is prepared to really work. A recommendation might then be that the factors indicating doubt about the leadership's commitment be analyzed and prospects studied in more depth before a decision to proceed is taken. Or the president of the organization may be perceived as "terrific," but his administrative backup is seen as weak. The recommendation obviously would be to strengthen the administration. Or a sufficient number of "big gift" prospects may have been identified in the study process, but not enough of them are ready for solicitation within the proposed timetable. The recommendation might be to suitably revise the timetable to allow for the necessary cultivation time through, say, a phased approach to the campaign.

Obviously, numerous variables are at work in each instance, and recommendations have to take these as well as the actual study findings fully into account. Concrete recommendations should be made in *every* principal area of the study's findings.

PART III: THE PLAN OF ACTION

The plan of action presents the general goals and requirements for the fund-raising program. Chief among these are:

Program specifications, including (1) a definition and plan for the "spade work" and prospect cultivation required to motivate support at the various gift levels, as well as a determination of the amount to be sought through public subscription and the means by which to accomplish this; (2) a definition of the general character of the effort; (3) financial targets for categories of support; (4) the number and range of gifts required, and (5) specific fund-raising policies.

Plan of organization. The organization is often best depicted graphically by means of charts, with descriptive material indicating the specific functions of the committees and their chairpersons and the number of committee members to be recruited.

Timing. The scheduling, sequencing, and phasing of a fund-raising program is of crucial importance to its success. The plan of action outlines timing, taking into consideration (1) competing development efforts, (2) the local fund-raising "climate," (3) the most favorable time(s) of year for fund raising, (4) the optimum time for the campaign kickoff and announcement of the campaign goal, and (5) the best time periods for each solicitation phase.

Public relations. This important subject is discussed in Chapter

7. The plan of action is concerned with (1) methods of publicizing the institution and its purposes, service to its community, and general "case," as well as promoting the campaign and its specific goals; (2) requirements for printed materials, presentations, audiovisuals, advertising, special events, and so forth; (3) the way in which responsibility for public relations activities relating to the fund-raising program will be assigned among the appropriate offices (development, public relations, communications, and so on).

Budget. The estimated cost of the fund-raising program, based on an evaluation of in-house resources, the planned use of professional fund-raising counsel, and so forth, is included in the plan of action.

The Study "Experience"

A market-research or "feasibility" study can have a profound effect on a not-for-profit organization's day-to-day and long-term development activities and planning. The information and insights obtained, and participation in the process of gathering it, often compel trustees, administration, faculty, medical staff, and other insiders to look at the institution, its relation to the community it serves, and their own relation to it in new and different ways. The experience can thus have a salutary effect which extends beyond the specific study report findings, recommendations, and plan for a fund-raising program. Since strengths and weaknesses are identified and evaluated dispassionately, the institution gains a better sense of areas that need strengthening, and perhaps a keener appreciation of those already strong. And the heightened sense of awareness and involvement which often results from the study experience helps the organization prepare for the arduous but exciting task of planning, organizing, and implementing a major fund-raising program, in whose goals and validity it must have full confidence.

5

Procedures

The successful planning, operation, and management of a short- or long-term capital campaign or other institutional development effort requires the application of certain well-tested and proven procedures that constitute what might be called a basic operating approach.

It should be emphasized that each procedural step must be tailored realistically to the resources, goals, and needs of the particular institution and campaign in question. While this chapter is primarily concerned with the operating procedures involved in a "typical" capital campaign, many of the basics have equal, and obvious, application to annual and deferred giving programs and, in certain instances, general institutional development.

Planning and Scheduling

As made clear in earlier chapters, a basic institutional development master plan is a prerequisite to specific fund-raising action. A similar plan must also be developed for each of these efforts, reflecting the goals of the master development plan and, in most cases, the findings of a "feasibility study" designed to test the institution's potential to realize whatever portions of the master plan's objectives have been selected for a specific capital or other campaign effort. The campaign master plan's basic components include (a) an articulation of overall campaign policies, compatible with the institution's broad policies; (b) a comprehensive campaign organization chart; (c) a complete table of needed gifts; (d) campaign job descriptions; (e) quotas for soliciting committees, and (f) a campaign budget and operating schedule.

The campaign master plan is usually the product of intensive evaluation of the findings of the feasibility study by the institution's board and its administrative and volunteer leadership, in consultation, typically, with the fund-raising firm which conducted the study and made subsequent recommendations and, if a different firm is selected to conduct the campaign, the senior officer and program director it has assigned.

The outcome of these cogitations—sometimes the planning group within the institution is given a name like the "Institutional Planning Committee"—should be a thorough, meticulously worked-out plan of action reflecting "input" of the trustees, administration, and professional counsel in the context of the findings of the feasibility study. Consensus that this plan, and only this plan, shall constitute the basic strategy outline for the campaign is essential at the outset, although of course changing conditions or unexpected developments may require minor or even major modifications once the campaign is under way. Whenever some inconsistency or flat contradiction in logic or efficacy in the basic plan is revealed, this almost always is an indication that the plan as originally formulated was not sound, not clearly understood by all who were responsible for it, or based on incomplete information. It goes without saying that such mistakes are costly in terms of the time and effort of all concerned and can have catastrophic effects on campaign scheduling. They must be recognized early and corrected.

Scheduling, or devising a campaign timetable, is an essential part of every sound campaign plan. Indeed, it is possible to view the campaign plan itself as a highly detailed timetable for action. This schedule indicates all major campaign events and goals and the points at which, on a month-by-month basis, they must be accomplished. It is self-evident that a major change in any phase of the timetable will affect the remaining phases; when such a change becomes necessary, the entire campaign calendar should be redrawn as the result of a genuine "thinking-through" process. It is true that in most instances subsequent phases will reappear at approximately the same intervals, but this is not always the case. A major determinant, of course, is the nature of whatever factor(s) required the change to begin with, and their effect on timing and other aspects of the campaign.

The advantages of a tightly drawn campaign calendar that is closely adhered to and intelligently modified as necessary are obvious. It assures that all the procedural steps in the campaign occur in the correct sequence and that all concerned are aware of what that sequence is and what is required of them at which point; it provides a ready means for gauging progress (or slippage, should that occur); and it serves as a motivating and rallying point for institutional leadership and the volunteer organization.

A final note: there are no real shortcuts in fund raising. A capital campaign has many objectives, of which the goal of raising a given sum of money is the primary, but not only, one. A capital campaign is, or should be, a building process in which the institution seeks not only to reach a specific fund-raising dollar goal, but to "position" itself for more effective, across-the-board institutional development for the future.

The Pivotal Role of Institution Leadership

An institution's governing body should be prepared to demonstrate its support of a fund-raising program by making proportionately generous contributions and by agreeing to devote the time and energy necessary to assure the campaign's success. These basic assumptions, in fact, underlie every soundly planned campaign effort. Aside from its other obvious benefits, support by top volunteer and administrative leadership is a clear signal to in-institution groups and individuals, as well as the outside world, that the organization means business. Such support should be made visible and tangible in as many ways as a particular situation allows. Often, a resolution is prepared expressing the board's support of the campaign's purposes and goals, and its willingness to provide a specified level of financial support. Such a resolution should swiftly be followed by formation of a trustee and/or "nucleus fund" and, subsequently, organized means by which other groups in the institution's "family"—administration, medical staff, alumni, service employees, and volunteers—may express their support of the campaign.

Recruiting Campaign Leadership

The principles of sequential fund raising referred to in Chapter 2 can effectively be applied to leadership recruitment in many, although not all, cases. The campaign steering committee, sometimes called the ad hoc leadership selection committee, which is organized by institutional leadership working with the campaign program director, normally includes a nucleus of trustees and individuals in the business community with clear top-level leadership potential. This group has responsibility for recruiting the campaign chairman and for coordinating the early stages of the campaign.

Success in enlisting top campaign leadership depends on certain obvious factors. It is essential to explain clearly to all prospective candidates the precise nature of the job they are being asked to take on, the amount of time it will require, who their associates are likely to be, how they will interrelate (illustrated best by a simple organization chart), and so on. In some cases it is not possible to arrive at a choice for campaign chairman acceptable to the majority of steering committee members (or, of course, a consensus prospect may decline). An effective alternative can be the use of the team approach. The top campaign team would include the campaign chairman, co-chairmen (perhaps pairing an "elder statesman" as chairman with a younger executive vice chairman), and, usually, top administrators. It is important, of course, to ensure that the institution's entire constituency is represented among campaign leadership. This consideration applies not only to such obvious groups as the economic, social, and cultural leaders of the community and to faculty, medical staff, employees, parents, alumni, minorities, and so on, but also to any institutions which are related to, or affiliated with, the institution planning the campaign.

Once a campaign chairman, or campaign co-chairmen, have been selected, the same basic approach is applied sequentially to recruiting volunteer leadership at all remaining levels, according to the campaign master plan. The ability to produce effective leadership (and suitable "pace-setting" leadership gifts, of which more later) is the acid test of whether the board of trustees is serious and the campaign and its goals have significant appeal.

Public Relations

Communicating accurately and persuasively the goals and purposes of the campaign and indicating the individuals and organizations providing leadership and support are essential to getting the effort under way once leadership is in place. The more common means by which these ends are achieved will be considered here.

Most professionally prepared feasibility study reports include a publicity plan and an outline of public relations goals as these relate to a capital or annual campaign, project fund raising, or other development program. As with the campaign itself, planning and scheduling are at the heart of good PR. Production schedules should be established for all proposed printed materials—which should already be itemized, in greater or lesser detail, in the campaign master plan. A second schedule indicating all planned public relations activities—special events, media relations, and so forth—should be prepared, again following the master plan and designed to dovetail closely with the overall campaign schedule.

Campaign printed materials fall into two basic categories. First are publications designed for use with a relatively limited number of individuals and organizations, typically prospects for major gifts and top leadership positions. This category includes the case statement, an often sizable document detailing all the arguments on behalf of the institution and its campaign goals, and presenting leadership, dollar goals, gift opportunities, campaign schedules, and other pertinent basic information. The case statement—or a summary of it which is sometimes called the key statement—is usually duplicated in limited quantities and used as a basic campaign document with the constituents and prospects indicated.

The case statement also serves as a valuable source for the second category of printed materials—those for which wider distribution is planned, as well as special presentations for project fund raising. Chief among these is an attractive printed brochure, incorporating the key points made in the case statement and presenting graphic illustrations (photographs, architect's renderings, and the like) of planned campaign goals. This "major" brochure is used as the basic campaign publication with volunteers, in gift solicitation, and for various campaign-related publicity purposes. It typically contains a table of campaign goals, representative gift opportunities, and campaign leadership names. Other printed materials include gift opportunities brochures or folders, guides about ways of making gifts, volunteers' kits, campaign newsletters or bulletins, and so forth.

Attention should be given to ensuring that both the case statement and various printed materials are carefully thought through and well executed. It is sometimes said a fancy brochure never raised a dollar, and this may be true—especially if the brochure is perceived as being needlessly lavish. But especially in the early stages of the campaign, it is usual to hear leadership and volunteers at all levels complain they have "nothing to show" prospects and that without comprehensive, tastefully designed printed materials that enable the reader swiftly to assimilate the main points under consideration and lend a touch of "interpretative emotion," the campaign is often perceived as lacking concrete reality. Although it may seem irrational, what these observations reflect is the simple human need to see it "in print," after which it becomes more "real."

Prospect Research

Carefully compiled lists of gift prospects provide the information around which all other campaign operations revolve and upon which, indeed, every important campaign function depends. The degree of accuracy, competence, and imagination with which they are developed, maintained, and used is ultimately reflected in the actual campaign dollar totals. Developing and maintaining prospect lists is a painstaking, time-consuming process. But shortcuts here can be enormously costly, and the temptation to take them must be avoided. Here are some—but by no means all—of the key characteristics of a good prospect list:

- All the prospects are listed accurately and correctly.
- All pertinent information is recorded.
- Duplications have been eliminated.
- The information is in usable form.
- Any prospect can be located, and his or her or its status determined, at once.
- The organization of the lists permits efficient coordination for various departmental activities and uses.
- Cross-references are clear and readily understandable.
- The list is stored in a format which, in addition to meeting these criteria, is also designed to serve the institution following the completion of the campaign.

Prospect List Development

However well organized and maintained, a prospect list can be no better than the names it contains. The first step in developing a prospect list is to examine thoroughly all pertinent existing records. Professional fund-raising counsel (including the program director) can provide assistance in this process. Once existing lists have been evaluated, the next step is to fill in gaps and expand all areas and categories to the maximum degree feasible. Sources for names will vary widely according to the type, size, age, location, nature, and standing of the institution, but in practically every case the following, in approximate order of value, should at least be considered.

- The list of interviews from the feasibility study.
- Donors and contributors to previous campaigns at the institution.
- Donor listings for other pertinent campaigns (including United Ways).
- Dun & Bradstreet (selective ratings), Standard and Poor's, *Directory of Directors, Who's Who;* pertinent professional society membership lists; club membership lists and social registers; surveys or listings of prominent individuals in industry, commerce, mining, petroleum, and so forth.
- Trade directories, chamber of commerce membership lists, lists of local business and industry.

- Purchased lists, available in various prospect categories.
- Federal and state government publications.
- For small community institutions, voter lists, city directories and tax lists, three-car families, telephone book "classified" sections, and, finally, the telephone listings.

Probably the most important consideration in compiling useful prospect lists is establishing and maintaining absolute accuracy. This must be done from the very outset, and if it is, much time lost in rechecking and reconfirmation can be avoided. An error made in the listing at the outset can—and has been known to on more than one occasion, sometimes with embarrassing results— be copied and "stick" throughout an entire campaign. Today, the computer is playing an increasingly important role in this and other aspects of fund raising. This subject is covered in Chapter 12, "Data Processing."

Obviously, developing effective prospect lists also requires knowledge, judgment, and experience. These will exist to a varying degree among the institutional campaign leadership, volunteer workers, and so forth. The program director can play an important part in helping establish categories and priorities among and within the various list groups, although obviously his success here will depend on the accuracy of the information he is given by those most familiar with the community. What this boils down to is the need for campaign leadership to be prepared to spend considerable amounts of time on prospect list refinement.

Rating Prospects

Accurately evaluating the gift potential of each prospect is of obvious importance; when the sequential fund-raising process is used, it is essential, as the process depends upon knowing in advance the ability and willingness of prospects to give at various levels.

The most common sources of information for rating prospects are known gifts to the institution itself and similar causes or appeals, earning statements which can be found in an organization's various financial statements, and personal knowledge of the prospect, including intelligent estimates of individual assets and income. The last in many ways are the most important, since they also imply some sense of the prospect's willingness to give.

Prospect screening, or reducing large numbers of names to manageable sizes, usually precedes prospect rating, which is a more selective process. A prospect research unit is generally established, with the purpose of gathering pertinent data on prospects in each giving category. While individual rating is often unavoidable, rating by committee is a more refined approach which can eliminate snap judgments and prejudiced opinions. Although leaders do infrequently balk at the idea of evaluating prospects in terms of their giving potential, experience shows that most individual, foundation, and corporate prospects actually welcome suggested contribution levels. Of course, these must be realistic, based on accurate research and intelligent rating. Asking for too large or too small a gift can be highly counterproductive.

In instances where specific prospect information is not available, the formula approach is often applied. This consists of selectively rating prospects A, B, C, or D, according to the range of gifts it is expected each can make, and then translating the classifications into dollar figures ($10,000–$25,000; $25,000–$50,000; and so forth). This process, of course, gives the same dollar rating to all prospects in each classification. As a general rule, it is essential that the program director participate personally in the research of the top 100 to 200 prospects, from whom typically as much as 85 percent of the money to be raised must come. Obviously, the program director must work closely with top campaign leadership in rating this highly critical group. The accuracy of these ratings, more than any single other factor, will establish the level of gifts which set the pace for the campaign.

Cultivation and Solicitation

Turning prospects into donors is the "bottom line" in any fund-raising effort, and again, the application, in orderly sequence, of proven techniques will be highly effective in most cases if the preliminary planning, scheduling, and research have been well executed. Here are some key rules of thumb relating to the solicitation process:

- An institution that seeks funds from all sources—individuals, commerce and industry, foundations, and government—has the best chance of success.
- The individual(s) most likely to obtain the largest possible gift from a given prospect should be assigned to solicit that prospect.
- The solicitor's "status" should be equal, or superior, to that of the prospect. (Consideration should be given to the use of solicitation "teams.")
- All prospects should be familiar with the institution's case and needs before being asked to participate.
- Campaign workers must know each prospect's giving potential; often, the prospect will ask what he is expected to give, and the response—phrased as a "hope"—should always be the maximum, rather than the minimum, figure.
- Most donors will give more if they know they may spread their gift over a period of years.
- Presentations should be tailored to the prospect's known or supposed interests, with supportive information in the form of charts, tables, architects' drawings, or floor plans ready. The opportunity for a gift to memorialize the donor or an individual of his or her choice should never be overlooked.
- Intimate, personal functions, arranged for small groups of potentially large donors, are far more effective than larger public "special events."

The sequential fund-raising process, originated by Brakeley, John Price Jones and described in Chapter 2, is generally the most effective approach in a capital campaign. The sequential process has been shown to raise donor sights and maximize giving. It allows each prospect in each gift category to be treated as an "individual campaign" and helps ensure that all prospects are approached. Its success, as noted earlier, depends on the willingness to adhere strictly to the basic principles on which it rests. In terms of a capital campaign, these include the following:

First-echelon prospects—from whom the largest gifts are expected—will determine the "pace" or level of giving for the subordinate echelons and, in turn, the trustee and/or nucleus fund and leadership gifts committee sets the pace for the first-echelon category. Every member of the institution's governing board should be urged to give as early and generously as possible, the usual goal for this group being between 15 and 25 percent of the total campaign dollar goal. Because it represents a commitment by the institution's leaders and gives the campaign its impetus, the significance of nucleus fund gifts extends beyond their already sizable dollar value. Failure to achieve the targeted giving level from the trustees can seriously jeopardize the success of the entire campaign. Solicitation of other first-echelon prospects follows (or overlaps) the initial effort with the trustees. All first-echelon prospects should be approached on a personal, face-to-face basis, and the need for good judgment as to the most suitable solicitor(s), time, place, and so forth, is self-evident.

Second-echelon prospects are those who are able to give what are often called "major" gifts, somewhat below the level of the first-echelon contributions but nevertheless significant in amount and impact on the campaign. In large capital campaigns in which thousands of prospects are to be approached, the second-echelon category is often subdivided.

Third-echelon prospects include a variety of potential donor categories, such as "special," "commerce and industry," "trade groups," "small businesses," "local or district," "selected areas," "executive and professional," "community," and "residential." In most cases, informative campaign material is mailed to the prospect and followed up by a committee member's personal call. Door-to-door solicitation and direct mail are often employed to cover general prospects.

In conclusion, it should be noted that this overview of cultivation and solicitation—topics about which whole books could be written—is necessarily abbreviated, and that while the principles outlined apply generally, they must be intelligently and imaginatively varied according to the kind of campaign and the institution's particular situation. To take just one example, in a college or university campaign, alumni annual giving will often be credited to the capital-campaign goal, a strategy which of course requires clear explanation.

Acknowledging, Recording, and Receipting

These procedures are essential elements of a successful, professionally run capital campaign. The importance of suitably acknowledging each and every gift cannot be overemphasized. Perhaps the best approach to acknowledging is not merely to regard it as a necessary courtesy, but as a businesslike and pragmatic way of ensuring that donors at all levels will retain the enthusiasm and commitment to the institution which led them to make a gift to the current campaign. Remember: every donor is a prime prospect for the institution's next fund-raising effort, and often for other aspects of its overall development program. In this sense, a "satisfied donor" is as important to a not-for-profit institution as a satisfied customer is to a commercial enterprise. The fiscal aspects of fund-raising and capital-campaign procedures are covered in Chapter 8.

6
Professional Staff

Though often overlooked, or at least taken for granted, a charitable organization's professional development staff is obviously a major factor in the organization's success—or lack of success—in its fund-raising efforts. The qualifications for a development director or vice president for development are described at some length in Chapter 1 in the section "Within the Institution: The Development Office," to which the reader is referred. As that description makes clear, an "ideal" development officer is a rather exceptional person, and the demand for such individuals greatly exceeds the supply.

The result is that, in many organizations, the development staff falls in one way or another considerably short of the ideal. (This observation no doubt is equally true for many other professions.) Still, the questions remain: how can not-for-profit organizations find, attract, and retain the best possible professional staff? What sources for such personnel exist? How can candidates best be evaluated? On what basis should selections be made? How can the institution provide opportunities for on-the-job training that will result in more capable professional staff? While these questions, on the whole, have no hard and fast answers, an examination of them nevertheless yields useful information and helps bring the basic requirements for professional development staff into sharper focus.

Motivation

Keeping the more common motivating factors in mind can be useful in identifying, interviewing, hiring, and training professional development staff. Whether it is called "institutional advancement," "development," or "fund raising," effective administrators and staff responsible for this vital facet of a not-for-profit organization's operation and management almost certainly *must* be motivated, to a greater or lesser extent, by a real belief in the value of the institution's work and a desire to assist in enhancing or expanding it by seeking and attracting the requisite funding. To approach it from another point of view, professional development staff (with few exceptions) are not highly paid and may be assumed to choose the profession at least in part for the reasons just given.

Another closely related factor undoubtedly is a preference for work in an "institutional" as opposed to a "business" setting, for a variety of personal reasons. Also, and obviously, the development office will attract individuals whose strongest interests and abilities are directly or indirectly applicable—men and women with leadership and management and marketing experience; people who like people; people who enjoy research; individuals with public relations, writing, or media and sales skills, and so forth. Finally, the development office can offer opportunities for advancement within the institution peculiarly suited to the interests and abilities of certain individuals who do not find other avenues for advancement open.

Sources

Undoubtedly the best sources of experienced professional staff are, roughly in this order, other charitable and educational organizations, professional fund-raising firms, foundations, the media, advertising and public relations agencies, corporations, and, at the lower levels, graduates of the few degree programs in fund raising. Entry-level and support staff without direct fund-raising experience can be recruited from the same general sources used by other departments within the organization.

Identifying Candidates

At the senior level—vice president for or director of development, and, typically, this individual's assistant—the "grapevine" or "word of mouth" approach is probably the most effective for larger and better established organizations whose administrative leadership has access to, and frequent contact with, other institutions, professional fund-raising and public relations firms, and so forth. Such positions today are usually advertised in specialized journals such as the *Chronicle of Higher Education,* professional publications, the pertinent sections of *The New York Times,* and local papers. Executive search and employment agencies are also potentially productive sources of candidates. The usual factors and considerations that apply to the identification and selection of any prospective administrator apply to candidates for an organization's top and second-level development positions. When possible, the director or vice president for development should be involved in the search process for the assistant or associate director and will, in fact, frequently be a source of well-qualified candidates.

At the support-staff level, the procedures of the organization should be consulted. In some cases, the personnel office will do the looking, in others the development office. The possibility of recruiting from within the organization should always be kept in mind.

Evaluating Candidates

Depending on the organization's operating procedures, candidates will usually be screened first by the personnel director and/or administrator to whom they will report directly. Subsequently, in some cases, that individual's superior (usually the president or executive director, and sometimes selected volunteers) will interview the candidate. Often, of course, the senior development officer reports directly to the institution's chief administrative officer.

Evaluation should be based on careful consideration of all the pertinent factual data—the candidate's educational background, career experience, evident interest in and suitability for the job, references, and so forth (age is often a factor related to experience). In addition, the factors of personality and presence and the candidate's compatibility with the individuals he or she will report to, and supervise, must be closely considered. Although it seems self-evident, this point is especially important in evaluating candidates for an organization's top development position, because these "readings" will also provide a clue to how well the candidate will relate to and work with trustees, volunteer leadership, and local business and civic leaders. The development officer should, ideally, be as effective in his or her relationships with these key persons as the institution's president or executive director, for, particularly in a sustained fund-raising program, he or she may be one of the organization's primary contacts with these important constituents.

Selecting Candidates

Obviously, a number of complex and interrelated objective and subjective factors enter into the selection process. Aside from experience, perceived ability, references, presence, and personality compatibility, candidates should be chosen on a basis of the extent to which their strengths match the job's requirements and complement those of other development-related staff. For example, an organization that has a strong public relations department can better afford to select a development director with little experience in this area than one that does not. Generally speaking, such trade-offs will always have to be made, to some degree; the goal is to match them up with the organization's overall requirements and administrative and staff resources. It is not uncommon to find development officers—sometimes at quite large and prestigious institutions—with no previous experience in fund raising per se but whose background in, say, business management is impressive. To some extent, obviously, an organization is taking a gamble on such an individual, and, again, the variables of the particular situation (for example, is there a well-established development office, or must one be built from scratch?) will have a major effect on the final choice of a candidate.

Theoretically, the job description should "select" the candidate—and, if it is well written, it can go a long way toward doing this, at least in fairly obvious ways. Thus a position for director of development and public relations, or vice president for development and alumni affairs, ideally demands an individual with strong experience in both areas. But in the final analysis, most selection decisions are to a major extent subjective, and here, clearly, the abilities of the individuals making the final decision are also an important factor.

Mobility and "Raiding"

Generally speaking, there is considerable job mobility among senior and associate development officers, and as the comments in the section about sources for professional development staff suggest, job changing and "raiding" are fairly common practice— as in many other professions. It is not likely that any consistently valid conclusions about the likelihood of a candidate's remaining with the organization can be drawn from the number of positions he has held or how long he has held them, although obviously an individual who shows a pattern of changing frequently may be considered likely to adhere to this pattern. The ethics of raiding are, of course, highly debatable. On the whole, the question would appear to boil down to the fact that if institution A can make its development position more attractive to individual B than his present job at institution C, then institution A has the right to do this, and individual B the right to leave institution C— subject, of course, to the contractual agreements in force at the time.

Because of the particular and obvious suitability of professional fund-raising counsel to institutional development positions, and vice versa, reputable consulting firms routinely stipulate in their contracts that neither party will attempt to hire the other's personnel for a specified period of time. Actually, of course, a good deal of cross-pollination does take place—and, provided it comes about in proper circumstances, as it usually does, it can be beneficial to all concerned. Development staff with professional fund-raising experience are, other things being equal, likely to be highly qualified. By the same token, professional fund-raising firms know that an individual who has had experience on an organization's development staff will be that much more sensitive to client needs.

Professional Firms

It sometimes happens that an officer of a professional fund-raising firm is assigned to an institution, in effect acting as the de facto vice president or director of development, with or without title, for the duration of a particular fund-raising campaign or program. In such cases, agreements are reached between the organization and counsel; occasionally these permit the individual to remain with the institution (transferring to its payroll) at the termination of the fund-raising program. For the client organization, such an arrangement can at least temporarily solve the problem of finding development leadership while building greater capability within the development office.

Professional fund-raising counsel is also frequently consulted by organizations seeking development directors. Counsel's role will generally be limited to an assessment of the organization and its needs, with recommendations and the preparation of a suitable job description sometimes based on an audit of the requirements of the position to be filled. However, counsel can also be a good source of excellent actual leads, and this possibility should not be overlooked.

Training

On-the-job training per se applies chiefly to secondary-level staff, although of course the vice president or director of development and his or her assistant will also typically gain valuable experience. It is up to the administration to provide the development officer(s) with reasonable access to other members of the administration and the board, and opportunities to learn as much about the organization and its internal and external "constituencies" as possible. The development director, in turn, is responsible for training his or her own staff. Obviously, how and to what extent he or she does this will depend on the individual situation.

A professionally competent, secure administrator will make it a point to expose junior and/or support staff to a variety of situations that can increase their specific knowledge and skills and broaden their experience. Such an approach will help identify strengths and weaknesses at once and enable the administrator to better evaluate the roles that can be assigned to each staff member. In addition, just as many organizations encourage their administrative leadership to attend professional conferences, seminars, and meetings, so too does the wise development officer seek to expose promising staff to such enriching experiences.

The development administrator also sets the tone for the department in other important ways. His or her manner, appearance, dress, and speech should be a model for associates. Working patterns, including punctuality, accuracy, attention to detail, care in handling correspondence and use of the telephone, and general consideration and courtesy are among the important tangibles and intangibles which, as a part of staff members' professional experience, are also a part of their training. Regarding personal relationships with associates and staff, the accepted standards of behavior should, of course, be scrupulously adhered to; inappropriate conduct of any kind is particularly visible and potentially harmful in an office as exposed to internal and external view as an effectively operating development office almost always is.

Job Descriptions

Job descriptions for the director and/or vice president for development will vary according to the type, size, and location of the organization, and the extent of the job's responsibilities (that is, development per se, development and public relations, development and alumni relations, and various combinations of these). The following descriptions, then, are given as representative examples intended to provide a clearer sense of some of the ways in which not-for-profit institutions have found it most effective to define this important position.

As a rule, job descriptions for the assistant or associate director will be based fairly closely on the director's description, with the nature of the relationship between the two clearly defined. At the support-staff level, the usual pertinent criteria generally apply. Indeed, in many development offices support staff includes individuals whose responsibilities require experience and skills not widely available. One such example has been included here: the list supervisor, a position perhaps taken for granted (although none should be) but a key one in terms of the efficient functioning of the entire development office and operation.

EXAMPLE 1: VICE PRESIDENT FOR DEVELOPMENT
(for a private liberal arts university)

Reports to: President of the University.
Supervises: Directors of: Annual Giving, Capital Gifts, Governmental Affairs, Publications.
Responsible for: Planning and directing the University's external programs concerned with income generation and public affairs.

Basic Function

The Vice President for Development is responsible for the effective planning, organization, direction, control, and coordination of the University's relations with its various external constituencies through its development program, alumni affairs activities, and publications, including University press and public information.

Responsibilities

1. Work with the President and trustees in formulating an aggressive development plan with targets and goals on a realistic timetable.
2. Organize staff to support Presidential, faculty, volunteer, and trustee cultivation and solicitation of the following external support sources, on an annual, term, deferred, or endowed giving basis: individuals, foundations, corporations, and government programs on federal, state, and local levels.
3. Develop and maintain reports for information control and progress toward targets and goals, including recording and acknowledgment of gifts.
4. Direct all aspects of the University's development needs, in close cooperation with the President and trustees, specifi-

cally including the approval, supervision, review, or moni-
toring of: proposals to prospects, presidential endorsement
letters, promotional materials generated internally and externally, budgets associated with proposals, and indirect
costs associated with proposals.

5. Coordinate financial needs of faculty research programs, on
   a priority basis, for most effective external funding.

6. Work with trustees and other University officers to ensure
   comprehension of the budgetary process and the University's future financial needs.

Personnel Specifications

He or she should have:

1. Demonstrated success in directing and leading a market-
   ing-type venture.

2. A high degree of interest in working with a private educational institution and an understanding of the differences
   and similarities of management philosophies and styles of
   not-for-profit and commercial organizations. He or she
   should derive a personal satisfaction from raising money.

3. The ability to work closely with members of an aca-
   demic/intellectual community and volunteers.

4. The skill to evaluate the nature and significance of objectives and goals, translate them into a workable plan, and
   delegate as much as possible while retaining adequate control.

5. The capability to lead a team in the analysis of gift or grant
   opportunities and to develop a plan to capitalize on those
   opportunities.

6. The ability to coordinate promotional activities with fund-
   raising efforts.

7. Confidence-building characteristics.

8. Some fund-raising experience.

9. A proven record of training and developing subordinates.

He or she should be:

1. A polished, mature professional manager who is highly
   analytical, innovative, decisive, and tough-minded.

2. Organized and concise in thinking as well as in communication skills.

3. Comfortable with University faculty, trustees, administrators, friends, and students.
4. Strong and "inspirational" with volunteer leadership—without taking over their functions.
5. Persuasive with prospects.
6. Imaginative and creative in "packaging" projects for funding.
7. Sensitive to changing tax regulations and other gift-motivating factors.
8. Of the highest moral integrity.
9. Patient and perservering.
10. Willing to travel up to one-half time.

COMMENT ■ Obviously, this job description includes some measure of wishful thinking, as any good job description should. While it is unlikely that many candidates will be found who fulfill *all* the stated criteria, there are individuals who possess many of these qualities. Item 8 under "Personnel Specifications" of course rather gives the game away—individuals with the qualities enumerated *and* direct fund-raising experience are relatively rare. As a consequence, it is not uncommon to find organizations of all kinds, sizes, and degrees of prestige hiring development directors/vice presidents with little or no previous fund-raising experience. Although, as noted earlier, this does not guarantee unsatisfactory results, obviously, other things being equal, professional fund-raising experience is a highly desirable qualification in a top development officer.

EXAMPLE 2: VICE PRESIDENT FOR DEVELOPMENT AND PUBLIC RELATIONS
(for an urban general hospital)

Job Summary

Reporting directly to the Administrator of the Hospital, the Vice President for Development and Public Relations accepts full responsibility for a complete program of raising funds from private, non-government sources. He or she plans and organizes campaigns for capital gifts as well as mail appeals and other fund-raising endeavors designed to provide financial support for Hospital purposes, and administers all matters relating to the function of the Department of Development and Public Relations.

Responsibilities

Under the jurisdiction of the Administrator of the Hospital:

Departmental Management

1. Accepts full responsibility for a complete program of raising funds from private non-government sources.
2. Formulates, defines, and interprets fund-raising goals and objectives geared to the main goals and objectives of the Hospital.
3. Establishes policies, procedures, organization, and systems for implementing the various planned programs of fund raising.
4. Establishes policies and procedures for effective functioning of Public Relations.
5. Establishes broad open lines of communication for the effective transmittal and reception of information and ideas both within the Development Department and with other Hospital departments and officers of the institution. Attends regular and special Hospital departmental meetings.
6. Prepares the Annual Development Office and Public Relations Departmental budget based on an accurate analysis of the past year's expenditures and a realistic appraisal of anticipated expenditures for the coming year.
7. Identifies needs, recruits and trains staff (within budget).

Specific Fund-Raising Functions

1. Develops and writes a sound and salable appeal or case statement suitable for use with various fund-raising objectives.
2. Plans and executes an ongoing program of solicitation of capital gifts in the form of outright contributions, grants, pledges, bequests, trusts, and so on from business and industry, individuals and foundations.
3. Plans and executes an extensive ongoing mail appeal as well as solicitation of various other publics of the Hospital and the Hospital family, as deemed appropriate.
4. Plans and executes a limited program of assistance to those departments and persons within the institution soliciting funds for medical research, scholarships, and other non-capital needs.

5. Working with volunteers, recruits and trains fund-raising leadership and solicitation committees.
6. In particular and unique situations, solicits prospects either alone or in the company of an officer of the Hospital or a volunteer.
7. Through research, expands lists and files of prospects.
8. Assigns prospects to solicitors.
9. Receives from solicitors reports of fund-raising progress together with actual payments and documented gifts.
10. In conjunction with the Hospital's Public Relations Department, handles matters of public relations directly related to fund raising.

Writing and Design
1. Writes and supervises the design of all printed materials related to actual fund raising. These include: news releases, brochures, progress reports, fund-raising operational materials, mail solicitation pieces, fund-raising pieces for patient folders, and the like.
2. Writes letters (and suggested texts of letters) for purposes of solicitation, seeking appointments, follow-up, and so on. (Many of these are prepared for the use of officers of the Hospital and persons serving on fund-raising committees.)
3. Writes all communications emanating from the Development Office of a nature that cannot be effectively handled by the secretarial staff. (Many of these communications actually go out over the signature of the Hospital's Administrator.)

Office Management
1. Administers and supervises internal office bookkeeping and filing procedures.
2. Develops and administers internal statistical reporting systems.
3. Supervises the deposit, recording, receipting, and acknowledgment of all gifts received by the Hospital.
4. Supervises all written communication with the Hospital's donors and prospects.
5. Supervises the preparation of quarterly statistical reports for Hospital administration.

6. Administers a system of follow-up billing of those donors redeeming their gifts (pledges) over a prolonged period of time.
7. Administers the departmental budget throughout the year to ensure adherence to budgeted amounts for each area of expense. Also maintains budget file and periodically examines expenditures to date.
8. Handles all matters of personnel administration within the department, including hiring, terminating, and evaluating. Also annually updates job description for each employee.

Skills

1. Education: Minimum BS or BA degree from accredited college or university. Proven ability and extensive experience in institutional fund raising.
2. Experience: Minimum two to three years in institutional fund raising with good background in capital gifts solicitation.
3. Communications:
   Proficient and effective public speaking.
   Excellent writing skills.
   Highly effective at personal communication and motivation.
4. Office administration: Good working knowledge.

Personal Qualities

1. Skillful and diplomatic.
2. Firm and decisive.
3. Able to plan, organize, direct, and control.
4. Creative and imaginative.
5. Resourceful.

COMMENT ■ Given the wide range of responsibility delineated in this job description, a candidate should ideally have more than the "minimum two to three years" institutional fund-raising experience and "good background in capital gifts solicitation" called for. Since the public relations responsibilities are nearly as extensive as those for development, it is virtually essential to find an individual with PR experience if the position is to be filled satisfactorily. But the realities of the situation—that development officers with all these qualities are in very short supply—obtrude, and the institution indicates it is willing to settle for somewhat less than the ideal. One way of dealing with such a situation, should all the required characteristics not be present in the director, is to seek an associate director whose experience and skills complement the director's. For example, a director with good general fund-raising and capital-gifts-solicitation experience and an associate with a strong PR background could, in this respect at least, make a strong team.

EXAMPLE 3: DIRECTOR OF DEVELOPMENT
(for a small historical/cultural institution)

The Director of Development and his or her staff are responsible for planning, organizing, and managing all fund-raising programs for gifts, grants, and pledges from individuals, corporations, and foundations. He or she reports to and works directly with the President. In addition, the Director of Development works and serves as staff for various fund-raising committees and advisory groups.

His or her duties are to:

1. Manage the development office, including (a) selection, supervision, and evaluation of staff members. and their work and (b) maintaining operational and budget controls.
2. Organize a comprehensive coordinated fund-raising program for annual support, educational programs, capital projects, and endowment and special programs.
3. Organize and maintain a donor/prospect records and research system.
4. Identify and evaluate prospective donors vis-à-vis the projects and programs for which funds are needed.
5. Prepare and, when appropriate, assist in presenting proposals and grant applications to prospective donors.
6. Work with other staff members to ensure that all development publications are in keeping with the overall publicity/public relations posture of the institution and coordinated as to graphic design and style.
7. When appropriate, work with those preparing other publications to secure coverage of the development program.

8. Represent the institution to its constituents and public as one of its spokesmen.
9. Arrange special events and other activities designed to generate and foster prospect/donor enthusiasm and interest.
10. Submit regular reports to the President showing results vs. goals and costs vs. budget.

COMMENT ■ A realistic job description in terms of the skills and experience needed to adequately fill the top development position at a relatively small, specialized organization. As indicated in the first paragraph, the individual who accepts this job must be prepared to serve both as administrator and, on occasion, as staff.

EXAMPLE 4: LIST SUPERVISOR

Job Description
1. The function of the List Supervisor is a most important contribution to a long-range development program or an intensive campaign organization. Thorough understanding of the computer, and experience in its use, is essential.
2. One person, only, may be invested with final responsibility for the execution of this procedure, as tight control must be maintained over the confidential multiple files contained in the operation of a prospect and donor file system.
3. While the List Supervisor is responsible for the vital functions of the List Department, he or she must plan with, and work under, the supervision of the Campaign Director.
4. In situations where there is a Campaign Office Manager, the List Supervisor and the office manager work closely together.

Regular Duties
Supervision of:
1. Building and maintenance of all categories of prospect files.
2. Building and maintenance of committee and worker files.
3. Source library.
4. Research of prospects.

5. Flat listing of prospects.
6. Maintenance of muster list.
7. Distribution of flat lists and solicitation material and information to workers.
8. Maintenance of pledge cards.
9. Statistical reports of campaign giving.
10. Posting of gifts (responsibility for this may fall to the List Supervisor, depending upon a variety of situations and exigencies).

Qualifications
1. Filing experience—adequate typing ability.
2. Statistical experience.
3. Knowledge of research methods.
4. Knowledge of the community in which program is planned.
5. Executive ability.
6. Ability to work under pressure when necessary.
7. Ability to cooperate, with tact and diplomacy, with client staff.
8. Good health, reliability, good personal habits, and neat appearance.

COMMENT ■   This basic job description is applicable to a wide variety of philanthropic organizations.

7

Public Relations, Communications, and Special Events

In many key respects, professional fund raising might be defined as a highly specialized form of institutional public relations. The objectives are almost identical: to acquaint individuals and organizations with an institution or organization and its programs and purposes; to define the benefits it confers on the publics it serves; and, in most cases, to motivate those addressed to take some specific action. As indicated in Chapter 2, public relations is an integral part of any capital or other fund-raising program, and an essential component of effective long- and short-term institutional development planning and management.

This chapter will approach the subject of public relations from the special perspective of fund raising and will define the principal roles that public relations can, and usually must, play in professional fund raising. It should perhaps be noted at the outset that the considerable confusion which often appears to exist in the minds of institutional leaders about the precise roles of fund raising and public relations within their organization, and with respect to the use of professional counsel, is to some extent inevitable. Unfortunately, it is most frequently reflected in the failure at the top administrative level to coordinate the activities and functions of the development and public relations offices, a failure which can have serious adverse effects on the institution's fund-raising efforts.

Public Relations—The Image Makers' Images

The term public relations is used broadly, by nonprofit organizations as well as businesses, to describe the network of tangible and intangible factors and perceptions by which and through which the public—or, more particularly, those segments of it of greatest concern to the organization—views the institution, and which largely determine the public's estimate of the organization's value to society, effectiveness and probity, and its general "image." It must be noted, however, that the term public relations has also come, for many, to have a suspect quality, suggesting the manipulation, partial revelation, or even obfuscation of facts about the institution or organization. There seems to be a rather widespread perception that public relations is often in fact utilized by government, political figures, business and industry, and nonprofit agencies and institutions for the purpose of, at worst, actually misleading and confusing the public and, at best, performing a kind of self-serving, advertising function.

This perception, of course, is largely incorrect. Allowing for the fact that to some extent public relations does represent a *quid pro quo* proposition for most organizations, nevertheless it surely serves the public good in ways far more numerous than those in which it may occasionally work against it. Business and industry, in addition to their outright charitable contributions, spend enormous sums to sponsor a wide variety of programs in the arts, entertainment, sports, and so forth, which cannot precisely be labeled "philanthropy" or "advertising" and are, in fact, a manifestation of true public relations—an attempt to make the public think of the organization, and, preferably, think well of it, by underwriting the cost of some activity of obvious public benefit. Similarly, not-for-profit organizations typically make available, as a matter of course, a wide range of programs and services to the residents of their communities. One can examine virtually any private educational institution, museum, library, arts organization, health agency, or religious group and find numerous instances of its serving the public good in a variety of ways extending beyond its specific, chartered purposes.

This, then, is the positive side of public relations, and of course is a part—sometimes peripherally, sometimes more centrally—of the organization's case for philanthropic support. The function of the public relations office, in relation to these activities, is to promote and advertise them as widely as possible. Often the actual program ideas will originate with the public relations office, the development office, and other parts of the administration, as well as the offices and departments directly involved. Planning, implementing, and publicizing such activities is only a part of the public relations office's responsibilities, which also include planning and managing all aspects of the organization's PR program, working with the media—press, radio, and TV—and generally protecting and promoting the image the institution wishes to present by selectively promulgating newsworthy information.

Obviously, how well an organization succeeds in these efforts will to a significant extent determine its fund-raising potential and effectiveness. Sometimes fund-raising feasibility studies reveal, for example, that the publics on which a given organization must primarily rely for philanthropic support are unaware of its programs and needs or their urgency, or think of the institution as "that arrogant place up there on the hill," or see it as unfairly favoring one or another group interest in the community, and so forth. (Of course, such studies also turn up ways in which the institution is viewed positively.)

It can be said, therefore, that in this connection fund raising can often play an important role in enhancing institutional public relations, simply by identifying problem areas and creating an immediate need to address them.

Public Relations and Fund Raising

As stated earlier, this subject will be treated here from the standpoint of such fund-raising efforts as capital campaigns, annual giving campaigns, deferred giving and other such special programs, and ongoing overall institutional development.

In most cases, it is essential that the leadership of charitable institutions recognize clearly that it is theoretically, and indeed practically, impossible and undesirable to attempt rigidly to separate the organization's fund-raising and development efforts from its public relations and communications programs. Rather, what is required is a plan allowing for the imaginative meshing of these two closely related functions in ways designed to meet the specific requirements of immediate and long-range development planning. Figure 2, a typical organization chart recently prepared by professional fund-raising counsel for a major university, shows some of the possible interrelationships between and among the administration and the offices of development, public relations, and communications.

Fund-Raising PR: The Essentials

As noted above, public relations as it applies to a not-for-profit organization's fund-raising efforts can be viewed both as an extension and a specialization of its regular, ongoing public relations programs. If the institution already has a generally effective public relations operation producing satisfactory results, its development efforts are significantly enhanced. On the other hand, if preliminary studies of the institution's development potential reveal deficiencies in terms of its image or the accuracy and degree of public interest and understanding, a modified or new public relations program addressing these needs must be implemented before such fund-raising efforts as a major capital campaign can be launched. (The in-house development planning and start-up work for the campaign can, and usually should, be started immediately, however.)

Assuming a generally positive PR picture, the pertinent public relations elements of the master development plan and/or the plan for a particular campaign or fund-raising effort should be implemented. Typically, such plans will include the following PR elements:

Communications:
    Printed materials of all kinds.
    Films, slide shows, and other audiovisual materials.
    Advertising—print media, radio, television.
Special Events:
    Campaign kickoff events.
    Award and recognition functions.
    Benefits.

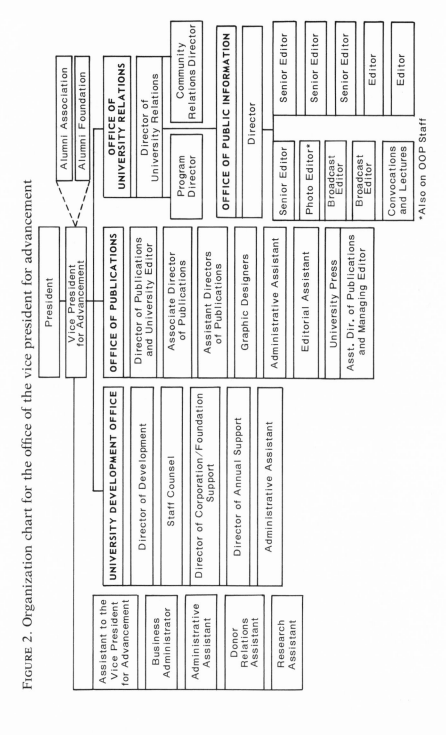

FIGURE 2. Organization chart for the office of the vice president for advancement

All these elements of an institution's fund-raising public relations program have relevance to outside audiences and constituencies, and some pertain to "in-family" constituencies as well.

Communications

The essence of public relations practice obviously lies in communicating a particular message or set of messages to selected audiences. The printed materials normally employed in a capital campaign include the major brochure, individually prepared proposals, special gift brochures, how-to-give brochures, volunteers' kits, tax leaflets, monthly progress bulletins, and so forth. Annual giving programs, deferred giving efforts, and so on have similar requirements.

The preparation and production of such materials must be supervised by the development office. (In the case of annual giving, the alumni office often functions, in effect, as the development office for this form of giving.) Often, professional counsel is assigned to research and write these key publications. In cases where the development office does not have design and production resources and/or experience, these services can often be most efficiently and economically handled by the public relations, publications, or communications office, either directly or on a subcontracted basis.

While the focus of campaign printed materials *must* be the campaign itself, opportunities to utilize other existing or planned institutional publications should be seized whenever possible. Often, for example, a college "view book," student prospectus, catalog, annual report, or alumni publication makes an excellent supplement to the major campaign publication(s). The same principle applies to the annual reports, magazines, newsletters, programs, guide books, and other publications of health institutions, religious organizations, arts groups, museums, libraries, and civic and social welfare agencies. Occasionally it is possible to combine two or more departments' publications budgets for specific campaign-related materials that can also serve other important institution needs, allowing for publications of a quality that would not otherwise be possible.

Films, slide shows, and other audiovisual materials often constitute an important part of the campaign communications arsenal. Needless to say, such materials should be professionally prepared whenever possible, although sometimes films or slide shows produced by, say, a college's communications majors can be highly effective for use on a selective basis. The same general comments about the preparation of print materials apply to audiovisuals.

Advertising can be an effective way of reaching selected or general audiences which an institution wishes to acquaint with its development goals and needs. A New York metropolitan-area university, for example, announced a major capital campaign with a full-page advertisement in *The New York Times*—obviously excellent, if expensive, exposure. Such advertisements should, whenever possible, be newsworthy as well as simply informative. The advertisement referred to presented the university's campaign leadership—an impressive cross-section of local businessmen, whose commitment to this cause was indeed, in its way, newsworthy.

A quite different kind of advertisement is the direct appeal, widely used by a variety of charitable organizations. Such advertisements usually seek to motivate the reader to make a contribution at once and, in this effort, are generally limited by the slender amount of information they can convey. In any case, such appeals are usually designed to attract a large number of relatively small gifts. A variation on this theme is the advertisement encouraging the reader to consider "investing" in the institution via a deferred-gift life-income program.

For nonprofit institutions, radio and television advertising is usually limited by cost considerations to free public-service spots, talk shows, and similar programs. Such materials and appearances should be professionally prepared whenever possible and viewed as potentially important components in the overall effort to make more people aware of the institution and its case for support. Such exposure can be especially valuable for nascent, small, and obscure organizations. The need for professional preparation of public-service advertisements is underscored by the high overall quality of most contemporary broadcast advertising. As with printed and audiovisual materials, the use of in-house production resources should be explored. Close cooperation with the public relations office is especially important in print and broadcasting advertising, for obvious reasons.

Special Events

Special events are an important part of an organization's public relations efforts and can play a key role in many fund-raising programs. Properly used, special events can heighten interest in and understanding of an institution and its goals and purposes; they can help dramatize a particular program; they can help build volunteer interest and commitment; and they can raise money.

Opportunities for special events are limited only by the imagination and energy of the individuals and organizations planning them—a good reason, again, for campaign leadership and the development office to work closely with the public relations office, on whose involvement the ultimate effectiveness of special events usually depends. Typical special events for charitable institutions run the gamut from annual meetings, anniversaries, award dinners, auctions, balls, bazaars, and building dedications to concerts, fairs, fashion shows, house tours, theater benefits, and so on, concluding with highly specialized events of local and/or topical interest, such as contests, film festivals, pancake breakfasts, covered-dish suppers, car-washes, wine-tasting parties, and so on almost ad infinitum.

Special events can be divided into several categories; the three primary ones will be considered here.

1. *Campaign kickoff events.* These typically include groundbreaking ceremonies, building dedications, and similar functions at which a capital campaign is formally announced. The top administrative and campaign volunteer leadership participates, and the event is often scheduled to coincide with some other important institutional function—an annual meeting, alumni day, or the like—for maximum newsworthiness. Obviously, it is important that the campaign kickoff be given the widest possible PR and press coverage, utilizing all available means and media.

2. *Award and recognition functions.* These generally honor prominent individuals in some way associated with the organiza-

tion, either for their accomplishments per se or for their achievements on behalf of the institution, or both. Such events include testimonial dinners, various ceremonies which recur regularly within the organization's calendar, and similar functions. The comments about campaign kickoff events above apply with equal force to audience and PR coverage.

3. *Benefits.* This category includes numerous kinds of special events intended to serve both as an avenue to heightened publicity for the organization and its fund-raising efforts and as an immediate source of actual funds. For some organizations, indeed, the latter consideration is the primary one—the annual dinner dance, art exhibit, house tour, or theater benefit is often the institution's primary source of regular philanthropic support. For large institutions with more highly developed fund-raising programs, such benefits, while raising money, usually have as their major purpose increasing the organization's visibility, underscoring specific campaign or other development efforts, and building volunteer enthusiasm.

As with communications, the initiation and planning of special events for fund-raising purposes normally comes from the administration, volunteer leadership, and the development office. Depending on its resources, the development office sometimes runs the event itself, usually enlisting the active support of the public relations staff and, when professional fund-raising counsel has been engaged, drawing upon its experience also. Since the primary purpose of special events is, in most cases, to heighten the institution's image, close cooperation with the public relations office from the earliest planning stages right down to the conclusion of the event is essential.

The Role of Public Relations Counsel

Depending on the resources of the development and public relations offices, some aspects of an organization's fund-raising (and other) public relations requirements may best be handled by professional counsel. When professional fund-raising counsel has been engaged, it is often able to provide assistance that reflects an understanding of the special relationship between fund raising and public relations, based on many years' experience. Professional public relations or communications firms and/or individuals are also available. Their orientation is usually toward PR per se, and to maximize results from the standpoint of the organization's fund-raising goals, it is necessary to assure that a clear understanding exists of the ways in which *institutional development* is to be advanced via public relations, which is not the same thing as promoting the organization's general image. On the whole, the comments and caveats given in Chapter 15 about professional fund-raising firms apply equally to the selection and use of professional public relations counsel.

8

Financial and
Gift-Control Procedures

Recording, receipting, reporting, and acknowledging contributions is a central and critical function of every not-for-profit organization's fund-raising activities. It has three major purposes: to ensure that donors are thanked appropriately and promptly; to facilitate record-keeping and reporting among the various departments and agencies within the institution; and to maintain the organization's credibility with respect to accurately and effectively accounting for, and using, the philanthropic contributions it receives.

While different institutions go about accomplishing these objectives in varying ways, depending on a number of factors, certain basic operating procedures are almost always followed, as summarized below. Because of the variations that exist among philanthropic organizations in terms of the purposes their fund-raising objectives are designed to serve and, consequently, their financial and gift-control procedures in handling philanthropic income, this chapter will present overviews of the systems currently in use in four organizations: an Ivy League university, an urban medical center, a regional chapter of a national health-research organization, and a children's social welfare organization. Interestingly, some of the relationships among such fund-raising activities as capital campaigns, annual fund drives, and direct-mail and other appeals will become apparent as these organizations' fund-raising gift-control procedures are briefly described.

Basic Operating Procedures

In one form or another, these steps, in roughly the order indicated, are followed by virtually all philanthropic organizations in recording, receipting, reporting, and acknowledging contributions:

1. Receiving funds (cash, checks, securities, and so on) and recording the pertinent information, including provision for maintaining confidentiality if requested.*
2. Transmitting funds for deposit.
3. Preparing and distributing receipts and/or acknowledgments, including personal letters.
4. Recording, summarizing, and disseminating pertinent information about receipts for internal institutional use.
5. Reporting pertinent information about nonconfidential contributions to the organization's "other" constituencies (donors, alumni, friends, and so forth).
6. Maintaining and using a "pledges receivable" file and follow-up systems.

Let us now briefly examine some of the gift-control procedures four typical eleemosynary institutions presently employ to carry out these essential functions.

An Ivy League University

All gifts to this institution are handled by its development office, which is headed by a vice president for development to whom the director of development, the director of annual giving, and the recording secretary report directly. The director of deferred giving, in this case, reports to the director of development.

Gifts are recorded and acknowledged by the recording secretary, who determines which contributions should receive additional acknowledgments, up to and including letters from the president of the university. Cash, checks, securities, and so forth are then forwarded to the university comptroller, and advice of

---

* Varying degrees of confidentiality may be requested by the donor, whose wishes, of course, must be strictly observed.

each gift is made to the appropriate quarter or division within the development office, often for transmittal to leadership and solicitors, as well as, when indicated, any other university department. For example, the library also would be notified directly of a contribution designated specifically for it.

When a contribution is received with the directive that it be split between or among various purposes (for example, a $1,000 gift whose donor directs that it be applied in equal parts to the annual fund, to the deferred giving program, and to a science lab), the recording secretary follows these directives, informs the departments concerned, and coordinates the acknowledgment process. Special fund-raising programs (such as one presently under way for the hockey rink) are also handled by the development office's recording secretary.

There are two major exceptions to this basic procedure: annual giving and deferred gifts. Gifts to the annual fund typically are received and acknowledged by the director of annual giving and his staff, with acknowledgments* made by the director or, at his discretion, the president, the annual giving chairman, class presidents, or others. The purpose of this arrangement is obvious: it permits the annual fund office to maintain the fullest possible contact with alumni throughout the entire annual giving process, from the appeal to the receipt and acknowledgment of gifts. The information received in this process, of course, is important in terms of planning future annual giving efforts. The annual fund office also provides assistance in transferring securities and the like, working with the donor's broker or attorney when requested. After being recorded and receipted, funds received by the annual giving office are channeled to the comptroller's office. In the case of deferred gifts, these too generally are received directly by the deferred giving office, whose director acknowledges them or arranges for a presidential or other acknowledgment. The gifts are then recorded, receipted, and forwarded to the comptroller's office via the recording secretary.

A central file is maintained for each donor to the university, showing all gifts of $1,000 or more over the entire period of his relationship as a donor. Presently, all this information is recorded

---

* Most major gifts cannot be "overacknowledged."

manually, as is typical in such institutions, and at the present time no use of the computer is being made in this process.

Obvious limitations of this approach are its labor-intensive aspects, and the inability to readily identify donors by categories—for example, all corporate contributions of $20,000 or more, and so forth. (The information can, of course, be obtained manually.)

An interesting and effective feature of this university's philanthropic gift-control procedure is its "gift book." This is an alphabetical listing, published each year, showing all contributions to the university received in that year and identifying the size and kind of donation. The gift book is sent to every donor to the university and, of course, serves as an in-house reference resource.

An Urban Medical Center

This 567-bed major teaching hospital is currently in the midst of a $9 million capital campaign, which is being managed by professional fund-raising counsel. The campaign office is headquartered in the institution's development office, facilitating the ready flow of information between those concerned with the annual giving and capital efforts.

Annual gifts are typically received by the development office and recorded in a card file (in the case of new donors, a new card is established for each). The check is then forwarded directly to the accounting department. A receipt and a thank-you letter, the latter tailored to the particular donor and size of gift, is sent. Smaller gifts are acknowledged by the director of development, while larger contributions are acknowledged by the chairman of the board or the president of the hospital. New donors are added to the full donor roster already on a computer list for annual-giving mail appeals, and all names receive a stylish quarterly publication presenting coverage of new developments at the medical center.

Gifts to the capital campaign are typically received in campaign headquarters in the development office, where they are recorded and a file card is prepared for each gift. These cards indicate the amount of gift or pledge and future payment dates, if any. The actual checks, cash, securities, and so forth again are sent directly to the accounting office. Gifts are acknowledged by means of a receipt, with a letter from the campaign office over the signature—depending on the size and nature of the gift—of the campaign general chairman, the chairman of the board, or the president. A strong effort is made to see that whenever possible, each gift has been acknowledged by a personal letter, with receipt enclosed, within 24 to 48 hours.

Reporting procedures are simplified, since the campaign and annual fund efforts are both handled in the development office, allowing for plenty of back and forth about contributions either program's director thinks of special interest or concern to the other. Since multiple-copy receipts are used for recording gifts to the capital campaign, it is possible to readily disseminate this information more broadly, when required. The accounting office maintains a ledger showing dollar amounts, number of gifts, and cumulative totals for the campaign, and this information is readily available to the campaign office. Finally, all gifts to the campaign are listed alphabetically, with kind and dollar amount indicated, in the medical center's quarterly publication mentioned above.

A National Health-Research Organization.

This organization is divided into geographical divisions; for this example, the New York City division will be considered. The great bulk of contributions are received in response to mail appeals, which presently result in peak periods (in terms of contributions) in the months of February, March, April, May, and June. Other sources of giving include special events, door-to-door canvass programs, and division branches. Gifts made to the national organization by residents of the New York City division's geographical area are credited to the New York division. The average gift size in a recent year was $25, and the division's total (including credits for gifts made to the national organization) was approximately $2.8 million. The accounting process of the New York division is computerized and is now being used as a model for other regional divisions converting, or contemplating conversion, to the computer.

All gifts received through the mail are handled by the accounting department and are first sorted into three principal categories: general gifts, memorial gifts, and legacies and bequests. General gifts are computer-processed by the name and type of donor—individual, company, or business individual (executive)—and each is given a computer code number. The computer produces a receipt at once for all gifts over $5. In addition, large donations are acknowledged by personal letters, as are gifts directed to a specific individual, such as the executive director. Advice of gifts of $200 and up is sent to the organization's campaign department for acknowledgment. A monthly computer update is sent to soliciting units, and a "presumed new donor" file is established for subsequent solicitation.

Direct-mail appeals, of course, reflect information updates in the computer produced by, among other things, the receiving/reporting/acknowledging process. Memorial gifts are acknowledged by means of a special memorial card, and the procedure outlined above is then followed. (Memorial gifts are coded when they are entered into the computer, for subsequent direct-mail "packaging.") Legacies and bequests, which usually are received from the donor's attorney, are generally acknowledged via the attorney.

Restricted and/or designated gifts are recorded and acknowledged accordingly (for example, "Thank you for your contribution to *such-and-such research*"), the designation being typed in on the receipt acknowledgment form. Computer coding enables specific interests thus identified to be followed up appropriately through special mailings and other programs. Larger designated gifts are also acknowledged by personal letters.

In addition to the obvious efficiencies in reporting, recording, acknowledging, and direct-mail list updating it confers, the computer can also be used to provide specialized and sophisticated information for a variety of fund-raising purposes—for instance, the names of all business individuals contributing more than $500, corporate donors over $20,000, $50+ individual donors from Staten Island, contributors to leukemia research, and so forth can be obtained in printed form on an overnight basis.

A Social Welfare Organization

Also New York City-based, this well-known organization raises funds for and manages a program designed to make it possible for underprivileged children to spend time away from the city during the summer, either at one of the organization's own camps or with host families in suburban and rural communities in the greater New York area. In a typical recent year, over 34,000 individual contributions, totaling slightly over $1 million, were received.

The majority of contributions result from direct-mail appeals, with mailings in September, November, February, April, June, and July. All six mailings are sent to each name on the list, regardless whether a gift has already been made in response to one (or more), on the theory that the mailings, designed to be educational as well as promotional, are worth distributing in the full sequence (but donors may request not to receive any mailings).

Approximately 1,600 unsolicited gifts were received in a recent typical year, totaling about $148,000, probably mainly in response to newspaper and other public-service media advertisements. An appeal included in a spring billing by Con Edison produced nearly 4,000 gifts, with an average gift size of $10, in a recent year; most of these were first-time donors. The total file comprises more than 80,000 names, of which approximately 62,000 are currently "active."

The director of contributions is responsible for receiving, recording, receipting, and acknowledging all donations. Until recently, all gifts were recorded manually on large file cards, which were then used for access by the various concerned individuals and departments. More recently, a computer service was contracted to convert the system to tape.

Gifts in the $1 to $5 range are acknowledged by cash receipts; all gifts of $5 or more are now acknowledged by a receipt which the computer produces, along with a typed computer letter. Gifts of $100 or more are acknowledged by a letter from the executive director and a computer receipt, as are gifts of securities, bequests, and so on. Consideration is presently being given to enlisting members of the board in acknowledging larger gifts.

The office of the director of contributions sorts donations by date received and then breaks them down into batches of

100–200. The names of donors who have contributed before are recorded via the computer terminal, along with the date, amount, and code for kind of mailing. New donors are entered in the same way, and a new account number is assigned for each. (A computer cross-check procedure is used to verify that first-time donors are in fact not already in the computer.) Once a month, the computer disks are sent to the computer service for a printout, which is then checked for accuracy by the director of contributions. At the end of the year, a cumulative, comprehensive printout is prepared, showing all donations received that year and in previous years, by individual. A contributor who had given each year since 1943, for example, would be listed for each year with the amount given; donors who had given some years and not others would be listed accordingly, and "lapsed" donors would be indicated. The listing also reveals anomalies such as a new donor who had given twice in the just-ended year at points falling between the "cracks" of the monthly computer recording/update process. At the present time, this organizaton is reviewing aspects of its gift-control operation, particularly with respect to ways to more efficiently utilize the computer in its recording, reporting, acknowledging, and mailing-list maintenance/update procedures.

9
Volunteers

Sociologists tell us that human beings have three basic needs: food, shelter, and clothing. These needs, however, satisfy only the physical man. What about the other natures of man—the emotional, psychological, social, and spiritual? To meet these needs, human beings want satisfaction, recognition, enjoyment, and a sense of accomplishment; they want to be involved as worthwhile contributors to a worthwhile group or cause. One way to fulfill this need is to become a volunteer.

The word "volunteer," derived from the Latin verb "volo," means "to will" or "to wish." A volunteer is one who wishes to give of his various talents to something he feels worthy of them. This description, down the line and across the board, in philanthrophy applies to every volunteer from a *Fortune* 500 chief executive officer heading a multimillion-dollar campaign for a major university, hospital, or symphony orchestra to a teenager on a "walkathon" organized to raise money for the March of Dimes.

Five key traits or motivating factors, however, can be identified that are common to volunteers at all levels:

1. A commitment (of whatever origin) to a specific cause or institution which the volunteer is prepared to meet through personal and often financial effort.
2. The desire to meet a challenge head on—and win.
3. A wish to contribute to a "common good."

4. Availability of spare time required to function successfully as a worker for a cause.
5. The ego gratification that follows after success.

These characteristics differ only in degree within any given volunteer structure.

The Origins of Volunteerism in America

The reliance on volunteers for a broad variety of charitable purposes is a uniquely American practice readily explained by this country's history and growth.

America has often and justly been described as "a nation of immigrants." (This is not a pejorative reflection on the only *native* Americans—the Indians.) From as early as 1607, when the first "official" colony was founded at Jamestown, Virginia, wave after wave of immigrants flooded the United States, and there was little ebbing of the tide until the second decade of the twentieth century.

These emigrés came primarily from what, before World War I, was known as Europe—from Russia and those countries west. Almost every one of these nations had a monarch as the head of state, and where a monarchy exists, there is always an aristocracy at whose whim and indulgence charity is dispensed as a part of *droit de seigneur*. (It is interesting to note that the three main republics—France, Switzerland, and Finland—experienced very little emigration.) These "new" Americans were fleeing from political, religious, or economic oppression toward the promise of a better life in a strange and often overwhelming country. Their unhappy past experiences with ruling classes, reinforced by America's inherent distaste for crowns and coronets, literally forced volunteerism into existence. Of course, some groups, such as the Jews of Middle Europe and the Nonconformists of England, brought with them a strong religious commitment to the concept of self-help, essentially the basis of volunteerism.

For reasons religious, cultural, or linguistic, and often for sheer survival, individual ethnic groups remained closely bonded together long after their arrival on these shores. Vestiges of this carefully nurtured ethnic identity remain even to this day in such communities as "Little Italy," "Yorkville," Lancaster County (Pennsylvania), and the entire state of Utah. As various groups of immigrants participated in the westward colonization movement of the nineteenth century, they established self-supporting institutions to care for their own. For example, the Jesuits founded a network of high schools and colleges to provide "bread and butter" education for the children of Catholic immigrants; in most medium to large urban centers, there is at least one Jewish hospital; and associations, clubs, and "orders" based on nationality (Loyal Order of Hibernians, for one) sprang up where there were large ethnic concentrations to provide a vast variety of services.

Thus, as the country became more and more hybridized, the scope and influence of volunteerism extended far beyond ethnic, cultural, and religious lines, and its practice has become a valued and indispensable element of the American economy, where contributed services and volunteer time are estimated to be in excess of $40 billion a year. More important, even, volunteerism has become a cherished part of the American tradition and national ethic, a fact which significantly sets the United States apart and makes it distinctly different from other modern nations.

Volunteers—Their Use and Abuse

In earlier chapters of this book, "leadership" is discussed in detail. The emphasis of those chapters is upon fund-raising leadership at the higher levels.

Top-echelon campaign leadership is, for the most part, voluntary; senior paid staff members, however, do play a major role, and the position of paid presidents is becoming increasingly popular (for example, both the New York Philharmonic and the Metropolitan Museum of Art have them, as do all universities). Although most fund-raising leaders are volunteers, not all volunteers are enlisted to be leaders. It is these "other" volunteers who are the subject of this chapter.

There is an old, semi-humorous axiom in fund raising: all volunteers should be selected on the "3W" principle of "wealth, wisdom, and work." Of course, this theory is not universally applicable. Volunteers for discussion in these pages are those whose primary attributes are work and wisdom.

MEMBERS OF SOLICITING TEAMS

Fund-raising leaders—the general chairman, the executive or steering committee, sequentially designated gift committee chairmen—cannot carry the total burden of a campaign or annual support program, however small. They need the consistent and reliable aid of a corps of volunteer workers—that "little group of willful men"—who accept the responsibility and share in the planning of campaign activities which culminate in obtaining a gift commitment from a prospect.

The "care and feeding" of volunteers is a gentle art that requires empathetic human (and humane) insights, bolstered by considerable skill in persuasion. The essential psychology to employ is to *invite* the volunteer to *share* in a *group* activity to *promote* the welfare of a *worthwhile* institution. A potential volunteer's interest can be deflected—and understandably so—if he is asked to *serve* on a *committee*. In such an approach, the human element is lacking, the worth of service is unmentioned, and the probability of boredom is virtually assured. Much is said about "volunteer fatigue"; this is caused more by underuse and *ennui* than by overuse.

Actually, the volunteer's responsibility neither begins nor ends with the solicitation. He or she has helped to rate the gift potential of the prospects, contributed personal knowledge of the financial status and interests of the prospect, and helped work out the best approach to the prospect. In short, the volunteer has been *involved*, in group action, in every aspect of the preparation that is a *sine qua non* of effective soliciting. Once a gift has been obtained, the volunteer is still needed to assure a continuing relationship, beginning with a personal acknowledgment of the gift. Once a donor, always a prospect—even unto the last will and testament. Genteel perseverance is needed—and will be respected by the prospect.

There is, however, another side to the coin. It was recently pointed out by the director of development of one of the nation's most prestigious and renowned performing arts centers that perhaps *too* much is expected from volunteers—involvement in rating sessions, planning meetings, cultivational events, and more. It is his contention, and one that he says has proved out, that volunteers achieve the best results if they go in after the internal staff has done all the basics, and simply do the asking. His view is that a fresh face at the critical moment of the "ask" is a welcome change and motivates the donor to make a more generous response. Both approaches are valid and can be used singly or in a combined fashion as an institution's needs for volunteer aid develop.

Whatever approach or approaches serve the institution's needs most effectively, volunteers can be of immeasurable value in the actual process of fund raising.

VOLUNTEERS BEHIND THE SCENES

Many people think they are poor fund raisers or, more precisely, poor solicitors. Their reticence in asking for funds could be motivated by a variety of factors:

1. They are painfully shy in close encounters of any kind.
2. They may be "gun shy" because of past failures.
3. "I'm a poor fund raiser" often means "I'm a poor giver."
4. They may have doubts about the worthiness of the institution and its needs.
5. They may have philosophical or religious objections to asking for money; for example, the Christian Science Church and Alcoholics Anonymous do not endorse any kinds of fund raising.
6. They may have some physical disability not generally known.
7. They become prime prospects as soon as they become volunteers.

If (1), (2), or (3) is their true reason for refusing, they could still have some talents or knowledge that they might be willing to share with an institution and could be used as "resource" volunteers—for "opening doors," evaluating prospects, low-key cultivation of prospects, and leadership enlistment.

Hospitals, art organizations, and political campaigns are today most frequently in need of directed volunteer workers—gray ladies, candy-stripers, volunteers for the information desk, telephone canvassers, phone answerers for telethons and radiothons, and good old-fashioned "envelope stuffers." Volunteers in these capacities supply untold millions of hours worth billions of dollars.

VOLUNTEERS AND SPECIAL EVENTS

Although most member firms of the American Association of Fund-Raising Counsel do not advocate special events for fund-raising purposes per se, there is a place for them, and they do have important public relations value. All too often institutions become insular and do not open their doors to potential donor constituencies. Special events, if well planned and, more important, skillfully carried off, can become two-way streets that can lead the institution to the private sector and bring the private sector to the institution.

Anyone who has ever given a dinner party for eight or a cocktail party for fifty knows the amount of planning and detailed work these functions demand. The myriad details require many hours of organized work: invitations and follow-up, seating plans, menus, flowers, "favors," entertainment, and more.

This kind of volunteer participation offers some glamor, particularly if the event benefits, say, an arts organization. And here is one of the keys to motivating and sustaining the interest of volunteers: enlisting those who have a known affinity for a certain philanthropic cause, those who have a positive emotional reason for serving a particular institution, or those who want to carry on a family tradition of philanthropic activity within a specific purview.

As de Tocqueville noted, the democratization of America, the ability to get things done, and a facility for organization, at all levels, are the country's unique strengths. Other countries do not seem to have the same ability to maximize contributed services in a cheerfully productive fashion. But organization is a tender subject; "guidance" would perhaps be a better concept. Volunteers cannot be ordered to perform or sacked if they do not. Nor can their time and talents be wasted because of inefficiency. In short, managing volunteers is a critical and essential element of successful fund-raising practice and merits the same degree of care and attention automatically conferred by professionals on other key aspects of their craft.

10

Charts and Forms

An important support tool in fund raising is the graphic representation—charts and tables and tabular presentations—used for various purposes in study reports, campaign plans, planning sessions, and volunteer/staff "education." More recent additions to the traditional family of charts and forms are the various "management by objectives," "perk," and other kinds of business-management visual presentations, which often achieve the same purposes, sometimes more effectively.

Charts, Tables, Forms, and Reports

Traditional charts show the basic organization of the fund-raising program, illustrating the structure, departments, and principal activities—in effect a sort of hybrid combining definitive functions, people, responsibilities, lines of authority, relationships, and timing. A word on the latter: as noted earlier, most capital fund raising today proceeds on the basis of "sequential fund raising" (that is, beginning from the inside and working out, then working from the top down in terms of organization and solicitations), and this applies, in limited form, to many "pressure" type annual campaigns.

Gift-range tables, particularly those showing the number of gifts required by ranges, and the range and cumulative totals of those gifts are especially effective in projecting the dimension of the campaign as well as the timing, because, again, the same basic sequence is followed.

For purposes of control and volunteer and staff discipline, and to show operational flow, illustrated operating schedules are vital. These are usually structured on weekly or monthly periods, listing specific activities to take place in the campaign organization. The "management by objectives" approach has much the same effect and can be even more effective for the single-minded individual, whether staff or volunteer.

Subordinate organization charts are used for unified, broad-based soliciting "divisions," and to prescribe and control research (leadership and prospect/donor), list department, and procedures for receiving, receipting, recording, and acknowledging all contributions.

To expedite planning as well as cost control and expense projections, budgets—almost always prepared in advance—are essential, and, furthermore, weekly or at worst monthly expense and commitment reports against the existing budget are vital to the integrity of any campaign. Such budget reports are also particularly useful in keeping volunteer leadership informed and feeling responsible. (It can be as important to know that a campaign budget is underspent as overspent, for this usually indicates that something is amiss and/or behind schedule.)

There are literally dozens of forms used in most fund-raising programs, including locator cards; detailed research and subordinate cards for prospects, donors, workers, and media; gift recording, receipt, and acknowledgment forms; transmittal and petty cash forms; leadership and prospect flat lists. These may be found to be already available at a given institution; if not, staff ingenuity should be able to produce whatever is necessary—sometimes partly on a trial-and-error basis until the best system is found. Professional fund-raising counsel, of course, will be able to advise on the kind and number of forms required by a given institution.

Statistical analyses, and the forms that make these easier to conduct and utilize, have been greatly simplified by the addition of the computer to the processes of research, prospecting and prospect recording, gift recording, receipting and acknowledgment, following up on payments and pledges, and analyzing gifts received according to factors such as source, size, cash versus pledge, soliciting committee credits, area and zip code, and, most important, by comparison to the gift-range table on which the campaign objective was based. Chapter 12 treats the subject of data processing for fund raising in some detail.

The *progress report* is a traditional form which most professional fund-raising consultants consider to be the single most vital device not only for control, leadership education, and discipline, but also for providing a permanent record of the campaign itself. Various forms have been developed, and the "checksheet" example reproduced in Figure 3 gives an indication of the range of information these important forms should report regularly.

Campaign Organization Chart

Basically, this is a graphic representation of the campaign structure, visually defining responsibilities and interrelations of campaign leadership, the various soliciting, public relations, and other committees, as well as their fields of activity, and as noted above, indicating to some extent the timing of the campaign itself.

A useful variation of and elaboration on the organization chart, which is most effective in giving volunteer leaders a quick overview of their responsibilities, is the inclusion of basic details of organization, such as financial quotas or targets, timing, committee and prospect members, and gift ranges, in enlarged boxes on the chart itself. These are often called "campaign specifications"; if properly presented and displayed, they are perhaps the most useful device for the quick orientation of volunteer and administrative personnel.

The thinking and planning which go into the preparation of the organization chart are the essential first steps in preparing a campaign plan. The basic problem here is that, once such a chart is presented, there is a tendency to fit people to the boxes rather than the boxes to the people, particularly under the pressure of the annual campaign. Since fund raising is essentially a "people" business, the traditional organization chart is a logical and effective first step, but it must be kept reasonably flexible to suit the

FIGURE 3. Consultant/supervisor checksheet.

Through personal review with top client leadership, company, and staff, and through examination of all appropriate documentation, the consultant/supervisor checks *progress*, *results*, and *problems* in the areas (or equivalents) indicated below. This should also help in preparing written trip reports and *biweekly situation reports*.

I. GENERAL
   A. Planning
   B. Scheduling
   C. Prospecting (continuous)
      Research
      Constituency question-
         naires
      Records (manual/EDP)
      Flat list/printout
      Staff screening
      Volunteer screening
      Rating
      Assigning
   D. Organizing
      Leadership
      Committees
         Trustees
         Nucleus
         Leadership
         Corporations
         Foundations
         Deferred gifts and
            bequests
         Alumni/patients/
            members
         Staff
         Major
         Special
         General
         Public relations
         Publicizing
   E. Soliciting and reporting
      Sequential fund raising
      Worker training
      Prospect cultivation
      Soliciting (team/single)
      Reporting results
      Receipting
      Acknowledgments
      Publicizing
      Follow-up

II. ADMINISTRATION
   A. Campaign plans
   B. Situation reports
   C. Charts (displayed? up-to-
      date?)
   D. Operating schedules (on
      schedule?)
   E. Office management
   F. Budget (including petty
      cash)
   G. Computer usages (EDP)
   H. Prospects (research, orga-
      nization, staff)
   I. Treasury (controls, charts,
      forms, bonding)
   J. Top leadership meetings
   K. Staff meetings

III. PUBLIC RELATIONS
   A. Plan
   B. Printed material (produc-
      tion dates, quantity, use,
      distribution, by item)
   C. Worker training
   D. Audiovisual, multimedia
   E. Prospect cultivation
   F. Press, radio, TV
   G. Special events (especially
      meetings)

IV. CLIENT
   (Relations and Frequency of
   Contact)
   A. Understanding of its role
      and responsibilities
   B. Understanding of coun-
      sel's role and responsi-
      bilities
   C. Internal (officials)
   D. External (leadership)
   E. Staff/reps' relations

Particularly, check program *progress* as related to operating schedules.

leadership as enlisted and, often, to reflect necessary adjustments in organizational planning and timing.

In a capital campaign, for instance, there may be occasions when a "citizens (sponsoring) committee" is desirable, and others when it is superfluous. In some institutions, public relations will be taken care of by institutional staff, while at others, a public relations advisory committee and a separate fund-raising PR operation are necessary. Gift control, or "treasury" (a term often used to describe that part of the process in which gifts are received, recorded, and acknowledged), may be taken care of by the institution itself; however, in some capital campaigns, particularly where the campaign office is away from the parent institution, a separate treasury department, often under an honorary treasurer, will be desirable, if not necessary.

At the very top level of the campaign organization, flexibility is essential, and the chart should reflect this. As leadership develops, there may be an honorary chairman, a general chairman, and co-chairmen, and there may be a desire to differentiate between a steering committee and an executive committee. It may become necessary to surround an inadequate general chairman, for example, with others who must have titles important enough to indicate their complementary responsibilities in the campaign operation. So, obviously, to properly represent the campaign internally as well as externally, the organization chart must remain flexible enough to adjust to these and similar changes, if and as they occur.

Various phases of the basic information presented in the campaign organization chart may be represented selectively by means of separate charts, such as the regional gift-phase chart in Figure 4.

Gift-Range Tables

As noted earlier, gift-range tables have a variety of purposes. First, in a pro-forma presentation, a gift-range table provides a useful method of testing reactions (as in a feasibility or market research study) of leadership and prospects to the dimensions of the proposed campaign, and of determining just where the prospect sees himself, his corporation, his foundation, his peers, and

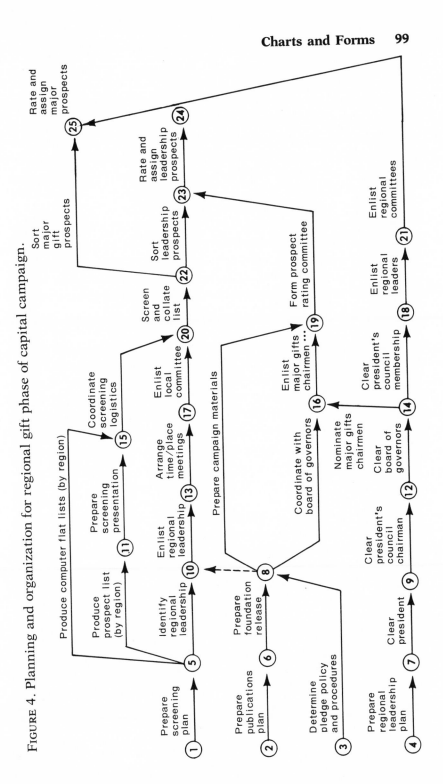

FIGURE 4. Planning and organization for regional gift phase of capital campaign.

others fitting into the various ranges described. Although this use most frequently applies to capital giving, it is equally valid for annual giving programs.

Second, after the market research study itself, the gift-range table is most effective in representing key findings of that study--that is, that there are, indeed, so many prospects for gifts of the various dimensions indicated ($25,000 to $49,999 all the way up to $1 million and over or, in an annual campaign, $100 to $249, $250 to $499, and so on). This gives substance to the report and encouragement to leadership, and it is on the basis of this kind of an analysis and presentation that the campaign plan itself, in fact, will be developed.

Third, a gift-range table represents a pattern against which later performance can be measured. Are the big gifts, so important in capital fund raising (usually the top ten or so provide about 50 percent of the money), coming in in the proper amounts and on schedule? If the table is broken down by prospect sources, are the trustees, the corporations, the alumni, the medical staff, the "grateful patients," the subscribers, and so on measuring up?

On a large capital campaign under way as this book is being written, the gift-range table reveals that, contrary to the findings of the preliminary market study, smaller gifts from alumni in "support groups" are accounting for far more, proportionately, than was originally projected, and that the big gifts are falling behind. Why? What should be done about it? In this case, the gift-range table is the most useful device imaginable for educating leadership to its responsibilities by demonstrating very clearly that there is no way any number of smaller gifts can make up for the loss of a few big ones and that, if the campaign is to succeed, they had better get to work on the big gifts—including their own.

Gift-range tables are developed on the basis of experience and the testing process of the feasibility or market study. Historically, and up to perhaps 1965, in capital campaigns the table was projected on the basis of the top ten or so gifts producing one third of the money; the next 100 gifts another third; and all the rest of the gifts the last third. Recent experience indicates that the top ten or so gifts are providing 45 percent to possibly 50 percent of the money; the next 100 or so, 35 percent; and all the rest—the smaller gifts, so vital for public relations, future bequests, resources for the future as well as for the money they produce—only 15 percent to 20 percent.

This pattern changes greatly for annual campaigns, but the principle is the same. It also varies sometimes on the very, very large capital campaigns (Stanford, Yale, University of Southern California, Columbia-Presbyterian Medical Center, Washington Cathedral, Andover, in the writer's current experience). The proportion for the very large gifts is somewhat diminished, but, again, the same principle applies. The gift-range table hence should reflect these variations, and ultimately, when all powers of persuasion and sources fail, it must prevail—and be adjusted to reflect the facts of life, even a campaign failure. Typical gift-range tables are shown in Figures 5 and 6.

Many so-called capital campaigns today are much more than that, covering, under one umbrella and one stated objective, all fund raising, from whatever source, for whatever purpose, and by whomever solicited. In effect, the major or larger gifts for capital purposes are solicited sequentially, but sometimes simultaneously with alumni, corporate, and other annual support donors; this calls for a complicated procedure, sometimes called the "double ask," at the upper levels. Thus credits are applied against the gift-range table at all levels, but, in the first year or two in the typical long-term capital campaign, there is more activity in the upper ranges for capital gifts and in the lower ranges for annual gifts, with the middle ranges coming along later in the campaign, and the final push on the smaller capital gifts in the last year or so.

The Operating Schedule

Essentially, this consists of intelligent planning scheduled by calendar periods—usually weekly, biweekly, or monthly—presented in some detail, showing the scheduled flow of important activities, stressing deadlines (screening and rating meetings, enlistments, advance gifts, opening meetings, general solicitation, committee report meetings, and special events). The operating schedule provides campaign leaders and managers

FIGURE 5. Gift-range table for a major university capital campaign.

Projected Pattern of Gifts to Raise $50,000,000			
Size of Gift	Number	Amount	Cumulative Total
$5,000,000+	2	$12,500,000	$12,500,000
1,000,000–4,999,999	10	15,000,000	27,500,000
100,000–999,999	40	10,000,000	37,500,000
10,000–99,999	250	8,000,000	45,500,000
1,000–9,999	1,000	3,000,000	48,500,000
Under $1,000	Many	$ 1,500,000	$50,000,000

FIGURE 6. Gift-range tables comparing projected and actual giving to a hospital campaign.

Projected Pattern of Gifts Required to Raise $600,000			
Size of Gift	Gifts	Minimum Amount	Minimum Cumulative Total
$25,000 and over	2	$ 50,000	$ 50,000
15,000 to 24,999	5	75,000	125,000
10,000 to 14,999	8	80,000	205,000
5,000 to 9,999	25	125,000	330,000
3,000 to 4,999	30	90,000	420,000
2,000 to 2,999	35	70,000	490,000
1,000 to 1,999	40	40,000	530,000
Under $1,000	Many	$ 70,000	$600,000

Actual Pattern of Gifts Reported as of Checkpoint			
Size of Gift	Gifts	Amount	Cumulative Total
$25,000 and over	4	$135,000	$135,000
15,000 to 24,999	1	20,000	155,000
10,000 to 14,999	8	84,000	239,000
5,000 to 9,999	36	198,000	437,000
3,000 to 4,999	17	57,100	494,100
2,000 to 2,999	26	57,600	551,700
1,000 to 1,999	29	37,010	588,710
Under $1,000	10	$ 4,100	$592,810

with the planned discipline which is so vital to the effective use of staff and volunteers.

The operating schedule is most effective when displayed visually, first in the campaign plan, and then in wall-chart form, where it can be clearly seen by all involved and progress or lack thereof graphically indicated. (This is equally applicable to campaign charts, gift-range tables, and that ever-vital list of the "big ten" prospects from which such a large part of the money in any capital campaign must come.)

The enlarged wall-type presentation of an operating schedule can effectively and dramatically show the flow of campaign operations, from A to Z and day one to day 365. This is often supported by a "management by objectives" type of presentation, which is somewhat more subjective, focusing on individuals with specific responsibilities and objectives.

Most such charts are broken down into these major periods: planning, organization, advance solicitation (at the conclusion of which the opening event and campaign announcement are usually scheduled), general solicitation, follow-up, and cleanup. These periods are shown running across the top of the chart and vary from a few weeks, and months, up to years. (While the usual annual campaign is accomplished in five or six months, the more typical capital campaigns today are running for three to five years, which means that the operating schedule, like the operating chart and the gift-range table, is in a constant state of evaluation and evolution. It, too, must be flexible.

Running down the side, typical subject areas are administration, trustees and/or the "nucleus fund," leadership gifts, major gifts, special gifts, commerce and industry, foundations, deferred gifts and bequests, public relations and information, and office management (including the list department), adjusted according to the organization structure, prospect areas, and local nomenclature. A typical campaign operating schedule is shown on the following pages. (A copy of it has also been printed on the inside of the dust jacket. It may be mounted for ready, permanent reference if desired.)

Budget

Financial accountability is a priority concern of every institution or organization raising money, and of its development staff and fund-raising counsel. The budget, prepared in advance and approved by the institution's board of trustees or its designee, is developed by categories and presented in a form against which expenses and commitments can be tallied. A typical capital cam-

PLANNING

SOLICITING COMMITTEES	1	2	3	4	5
ADMINISTRATION	Determine objective in relation to needs; set dates and clear with authorities; employ campaign manager and writer; get necessary permits; assure adequate operating funds; get headquarters space.	Secure lists supervisor; develop leadership list; set objectives for soliciting committees; build up basic prospect files; card all prospects; determine all personnel needed; borrow or buy needed furniture and equipment; select signing officers.	Enlist general chairmen; list sponsors to give representation to all groups of potential donors; make decision on solicitation of governments.	Enlist honorary chairmen, vice chairmen, sponsoring committee; honorary treasurer; make decision on use of canisters, tag-day, booth canvass; make decision on period of pledges.	Enlist chairmen for soliciting committees; enlist volunteers to work at headquarters with chairmen; and appoint committees on lists, meetings, distribution of printed material, follow-up, prospect cultivation, and canvasser education.
SPECIAL INDIVIDUALS	Select special men and women prospects (board members and friends, top executives).	SET ADVANCE GIFT OBJECTIVES Advance % Am't Men ___ $___ Women ___ $___	ENLIST CHAIRMEN AND CHAIRWOMEN Special % Am't Men ___ $___ Women ___ $___	Make decision on use of special presentations for key and selected individuals; review and refine lists.	Enlist vice chairmen and vice chairwomen if necessary.
GENERAL INDIVIDUALS	Get source material for prospect lists (other campaigns, Directory of Directors, church and fraternal organizations, social groups, friends, auxiliaries).	SET OBJECTIVES % Am't Men ___ $___ Women ___ $___		List potential team captains and workers.	Flat list all prospects alphabetically.
SPECIAL CORPORATIONS		SET OBJECTIVES Advance & Special Advance % Am't Special % Am't Men ___ $___ ___ $___ Women ___ $___ ___ $___		Review and refine lists.	
GENERAL CORPORATIONS	Get source material for prospect lists (Board of Trade, Chamber of Commerce, trade and professional organizations, classified phone directory, other campaigns).	SET OBJECTIVES % Am't Men ___ $___ Women ___ $___	Decide on categories of business if necessary (groups).	List potential group, sectional chairmen and canvassers.	Flat list all prospects alphabetically.
EMPLOYEES, CLUBS, AND ORGANIZATIONS		SET OBJECTIVES % Am't Men ___ $___ Women ___ $___	List companies and numbers of employees for canvassing.	Register with employee charity funds and clubs.	Decide on method of organization: business, geographical, or general.
PUBLICITY AND FEATURES	Survey on "case": photographs, charts, statistics.	Write major brochure; set up scrap book for clippings.	Major brochure copy cleared. Write preliminary case statement.	Major brochure to printer; order receipt forms. Write workers' handbook.	Releases on top leadership; print or reproduce preliminary case statement.
DEFINITIONS	**Preliminary Case Statement** Initial printed announcement mailed to most listed prospects about five weeks before solicitation.	**Major Brochure** For special prospects for larger gifts; limited distribution by mail for personal follow-ups.	**Mass Leaflet** General public use with smaller donors, employees' clubs, and organizations.	**Workers' Handbook** Printed or mimeographed piece for information of workers.	**Subscription Cards** With typed-in names of all listed prospects.
FUNDAMENTALS	Prospect—Worker Assignment Ratio Special 5–1 General 10–1 Residential 15–1 Employees 20–1	Prospect—Donor Ratio Special 2–1 General 3–1 Other 5–1	Prospect—Donor Ratio Personal Call / Telephone Call / Letter Special 1 2 3 General 1 3 6		Principles of Solicitation: Attention Interest Conviction Desire Action

ORGANIZATION   ADVANCE GIFTS

6	7	8	9	10	11	12
Cultivation of the "official family" (board members, chairmen, friendly top corporations) for key "leadership" gifts to use for effect on special individuals and corporations less familiar with the institution's needs; start typing subscription cards.		Mail preliminary case statement; type subscription cards; continue cultivation.	Arrange cultivation meeting for special men, women, and corporation canvassers; enlist speaker and arrange for opening meeting.	Mail major brochure to special prospects; set up meeting arrangements; open deposit account for contributions.	Cultivation meeting for all general men, women, and corporation canvassers; plan report meetings.	Mail major brochure to general prospects; start mailing receipt forms as gifts come in.
Cultivate key prospects for this period; type subscription cards.	Rate top 5 percent of all listed men and women; canvass top (3–4) known sympathetic men and women for key "leadership" gifts.	Assign top 5 percent of all listed men and women.	Distribute assignments and worker kits.	Canvass top 5 percent of listed prospects for more "leadership" gifts; launch major brochure mailing to these prospects.	Canvassing.	
Enlist men and women team captains; review and refine lists as sources of canvassers as well as prospects.	Enlist all canvassers.	Enlist all canvassers.	Canvasser education, tours, meetings for the next several weeks.	Rating meetings.	Assignment meetings; type subscription cards.	Canvass next 7 percent of listed prospects; distribute assignments and worker kits; major brochure mailing.
Cultivate key prospects for this period.	Rate top 5 percent; canvass top (2–3) sympathetic firms for key "leadership" gifts; type subscription cards.	Assign top 5 percent.	Distribute assignments and worker kits.	Canvass top 5 percent of listed prospects for more "leadership" gifts; send major brochure mailing to special corporations and top executives (eliminate advance special men above).	Canvassing.	
Set group and section objectives; enlist group and section chairmen; review and refine all lists.	Enlist all canvassers.		Set up canvasser education, tours, meetings for the next several weeks.	Rating meetings.	Assignment meetings; type subscription cards.	Canvass next 7 percent of listed prospects; distribute assignments and worker kits; send major brochure mailing.
	Set up group subscription blanks.	Enlist company chairmen with preliminary case statement mailing.		Publicity for employee, labor, club publications and house organs.	Speakers to large employee groups, clubs, and organizations.	Distribute leaflets and subscription blanks to company chairmen.
Releases on supporting leadership; plan poster contest; develop radio plans.	Delivery of all subscription blanks; delivery of preliminary case statement.	Progress bulletin to all canvassers; issue releases on committees; print or prepare group subscription blanks.	Delivery of major brochure; set up workers' kits.	Send progress bulletin to all canvassers; make delivery of receipt forms; place advertisements; build up publicity with feature stories (see employees).	Deliver mass leaflet; organize poster contest; continue publicity build-up; place radio spots, features, drop-ins in advertisements of local stores.	Send progress bulletin to all canvassers; distribute posters to local stores; arrange speakers for clubs and organizations.
Receipt Forms Sent by headquarters to all donors of $1 or more as acknowledgment and for tax records.	**Flat Lists** Columnar lists of prospects for general use or assignments to canvassers.	**Progress Bulletin** Periodically distributed to all canvassers for education and for development of sense of belonging.	**Worker Kit** All information, printed material, subscription cards sent as a package to canvassers.	**Canvasser Education** Training canvassers to know why the money is needed and how to go and get it.	**Prospect Cultivation** Educating the prospects on why the money is needed; building up for a bigger gift.	**Rating Prospects** Checking potential donors to determine their ability and willingness to give.
	Fundamentals of Campaign: Case, leadership, prospects, workers, timing, budget.	**Publicity** Press, radio, magazines, features, speakers' bureau, window displays, advertising, printed materials.		**Meetings** Plan date, place, cost, chairman, sponsors, speakers, lists, invitations, tickets, control, invitation mailing and follow-up, press, publicity, program, decorations, speeches, timing, seating, menu, acknowledgments, final cost.		

SOLICITING COMMITTEES	PUBLIC SOLICITATION		FOLLOW-UP		CLEAN-UP
	13	14	15	16	17
ADMINISTRATION	Opening meeting.	Report meeting.	Report meeting; clean up mailings; get budget report ready on all expenditures.	Thank all canvassers; return borrowed furniture and equipment; turn over funds to client; close all accounts.	
SPECIAL INDIVIDUALS	Follow up on all prospects.	Report meeting.	Follow up.	Follow up.	
GENERAL INDIVIDUALS	Canvass all remaining prospects; report progress to team captains as gifts and declinations received.		Follow up all prospects not heard from; clean-up mailings.	Follow up.	
SPECIAL CORPORATIONS	Opening meeting, follow up on all prospects.	Report meeting.	Follow up.	Follow up.	
GENERAL CORPORATIONS	Canvass all remaining prospects. Report progress to chairmen as gifts and declinations received.		Follow up all prospects not heard from; clean-up mailings.	Follow up.	
EMPLOYEES, CLUBS, AND ORGANIZATIONS	Opening meeting—canvass all employees, employee clubs, union treasuries, fraternal and service clubs, and church and social organizations.	Report meeting.	Follow up; clean-up mailings.	Follow up; clean-up mailings.	
PUBLICITY AND FEATURES	Publicity crest: posters, advertising, story on report meeting; discuss funds received to date.	Progress bulletin to all canvassers: story on report meeting, totals to date, and so on.	Worker recognition and thanks.	Close all accounts; thank the media.	
DEFINITIONS	**Assigning Prospects** Selecting the right canvasser to see the carefully rated prospect.	**Opening Meeting** Public event to publicize and announce the start of public solicitation.	**Report Meeting** Meeting of canvassers every week or so to report progress (a deadline device to get more work done).	**Public Solicitation** Canvassing all general prospects; peak of publicity.	**Follow Up** All cards checked and covered—some reassigned if not properly handled; clean-up mailing.
FUNDAMENTALS	**Watch Duplications:** In Mailings (interfile envelopes alphabetically prior to mailing); In Solicitations (as special men and special corporation top executives); In Enlistment (keep chairmen advised as to candidates for all jobs).				

paign budget and a budget report form are shown in Figures 7 and 8.

As noted, budget is an essential element in campaign control, evidenced through periodic reports (preferably biweekly, at worst monthly), plotting expenses and commitments against the approved budget, with copies sent to institutional and volunteer leadership. As with other controls emphasized in this chapter, the budget has particular value as a measure of whether the campaign is proceeding on schedule or not and, particularly, whether campaign management is profligate or behind schedule. As a general rule, a realistic budget, reflecting careful planning and based on the plan of campaign, should function within roughly 10 percent, plus or minus, of the approved total, usually allowing for

FIGURE 7. A typical capital campaign budget for a major university (for one year).

OFFICE STAFF		
Executive Secretary	$12,000	
Clerk/Typist (with steno)	8,400	
Lists/Records Supervisor	10,000	
Lists/Records Assistant	8,400	
Supplemental Clerical Assistance	3,900	
Fringe Benefits @ 15%	6,400	
		$ 49,100
GENERAL OFFICE EXPENSES		
Office Equipment and Furniture	$11,000	
Office Supplies	4,500	
Telephone	7,200	
Direct Mail	4,500	
Postage (not including Major Brochure)	3,000	
Meetings	7,000	
Travel	12,500	
		$ 49,700
PRINTED MATERIALS		
Case Statement	$ 7,500	
Special Presentations and a Major Brochure	20,000	
Miscellaneous	2,500	30,000
Contingency		15,000
Subtotal		$143,800

Plus professional fees and expenses if counsel is retained; if not, add compensation for executive staff, usually about 35% of total costs.

FIGURE 8. Campaign budget report.

Period ending: _____   Date of this report: _____

Percentage of time elapsed: _____   Prepared for: _____

Percentage of total budget expended: _____   Prepared by: _____

Amount of $ _____ goal raised: _____   Percentage of goal attained: _____

Expense Category and Items	Amount Expended and Committed					
	Total Amount Budgeted	Previously Expended	Expended This Period	Expenses Accrued to Date	Percent of Budget Expended	Unexpended Balance
Salaries Assistant director Research assistant and list supervisor Secretarial and clerical	$	$	$	$	%	$
Presentations Printing						
Special Writing Services						
General Expenses Office rent Furniture equipment Lettershop Office supplies Meetings Postage Telephone and telegraph Audit and insurance Staff travel and living Subtotal						
Contingency						
Total Program Expense						
Professional Fees or Executive Staff						
Grand Total (100%)						

some movement between allocations. Financial controls presume that all expenses and commitments over some predetermined amount (obviously varying according to the dimensions of the campaign) will be approved by a responsible official of the campaign itself.

List Department Procedures

The list department is responsible for preparing, distributing, and coordinating the information required for the efficient functioning of the various soliciting divisions. The basic organization of prospect files must, therefore, parallel that of the general campaign organization. The task of developing lists from a variety of sources, which are usually in different formats, makes it imperative that procedures be established which will avoid duplication of effort and, even more important, ensure accuracy and consistency in the tabulation of this vital information.

Ultimately, of course, this information may—and in many instances should—be transferred to computer storage systems; today, indeed, it is even possible to compile and/or update lists via a computer mini terminal. (The subject of data processing, including the use of the computer, is covered in Chapter 12.)

Regardless of what system or systems are used to store the information, the basic elements remain the same and include, among others, the following, described here for the sake of greater clarity in terms of the traditional card-system format.

Prospect files. The prospect files should contain a card for every business organization, foundation, and individual identified as an actual donor or a potential prospect or committee member. The master or locator file is an A to Z card file of all such, used mainly to locate the division of the campaign to which a particular prospect has been assigned. Subordinate or divisional files, color- or otherwise coded differently from the master file cards, are established for various prospect categories—individuals, corporations, foundations, and so on. Eventually, each subordinate card file will be further divided into "gifts received," "unreported prospects," and "refusals" categories.

Worker files. These follow the format of the prospect files, generally using the same master or locator card file with subordinate or divisional file cards prepared for each volunteer as he or she is enlisted. The subordinate or divisional file cards show which division or divisions each worker can be found in—individual, corporate, foundation, top campaign leadership and committee men and women, areas outside the community, and so forth. Subcategories should be established as required within each division.

Mailings. It is usually the responsibility of the list department to see that the envelopes necessary for mailings to prospects and workers are prepared in time to meet each mailing date in the campaign operating schedule. In addition to the obvious requirement of accuracy in typing names and addresses, the names in each mailing must, by whatever system is most suitable, be cross-checked against the prospect and worker files to avoid duplication. For example, a business executive may appear in the file listings under "business executive," "individual prospect," and "worker." Obviously, while it is important to avoid duplications, it is essential to ensure that each prospect and/or worker receives every mailing he or she is intended to get. Again, the watchword is care—and intelligent use of data processing resources and systems.

The Subscription or Pledge Card

Now we come to the most important of all the forms—the subscription or pledge card, which is, in effect, particularly for a capital campaign, a legal contract between the donor and the donee, with the former committing himself legally to make payments toward an overall pledged amount. For annual giving, where payroll deductions are sought, a different form provides this authorization; where there are other periodical monthly or quarterly deductions, the pattern of commitment is basically similar to the capital pledge form.

Early in many capital campaigns, where there are complexities in the donor's wishes regarding the use of the funds or methods of payment, legally prepared letters are often used, and sometimes these are supplemented by subscription cards. These, too, of course, are binding contracts, unless, as is often the case, they are revocable under certain logical conditions, as in "letters of intent." Corporations sometimes use this device, predicated on the intention of the corporation's board of directors to approve payments toward an intended amount over some period of years, but with no legal obligation to do so. Obviously, this decision is subject to economic and other conditions in the business organization.

Some institutions prefer to use subscription cards which make the commitment revocable and subject to the wishes and financial conditions of the donor at the time payment is called for. Most, however, are in the form of an irrevocable commitment, usually including such phraseology as "in consideration of the gifts of others" or the like. Some institutions have both forms available.

In annual campaigns, the subscription cards at the level of, say, a residential canvass are often bound into numbered books, with the forms themselves also numbered, thus facilitating the solicitor's accounting for funds received. Other annual campaigns use subscription cards with detachable receipts, which can effect important economies in recording and acknowledging contributions.

Considering that the subscription or pledge form is the one real contract between the donor and the donee, all too often the potential use of this form as a sales piece is forgotten. Since this is the one "form" that *every* prospect reads in the process of becoming a donor, it is obviously advantageous to have a short message about the case for the institution and/or any other vital information (as for matching provisions) on the card's back or fold-over.

The forms usually provide space for the amount of the pledge, terms of payment or down payment, purpose(s) for which the funds are designated, the printed name and address and space for signature of the donor, date, sometimes the prospect's last gift, the name of the solicitor, and so on. Where the "double-ask" is involved under the "umbrella" type of capital campaign, the form is sometimes complicated—or overcomplicated—by provisions for annual giving as well. Often there are also provisions for bequests, or for indicating interest in making a deferred gift. Obviously, the need for simple, clear graphic design and organization of the form's contents—requisites for every pledge card—increase with the amount and complexity of information it contains. Two examples of effective subscription cards have been reproduced here.

Traditionally, the subscription card is designed to fit into the usual #6 or #10 envelopes. On capital campaigns, however, it can be effective in ensuring that the card is always delivered and collected by the solicitor to make it outsized so it won't fit into a standard envelope, but into one specially made for it, or none at

&R

THE HOSPITAL OF ST. RAPHAEL

The Fund for
MEDI/
CENTER
1

Columbia-Presbyterian Medical Center Fund, Inc.
100 Haven Avenue, New York, NY 10032

All gifts are deductible for income tax purposes within the limits prescribed by law.

Checks should be made payable to:
Columbia-Presbyterian Medical Center Fund, Inc.

Securities should be endorsed in blank, or accompanied by a stock power endorsed in blank, and sent by certified or registered mail to:
Mr. R. N. Ott, Assistant Secretary,
... Presbyterian Medical Center Fund, Inc.,
New York, N.Y. 10032.

In recognition of the achievements of Columbia-Presbyterian Medical Center in health care, education and research; in support of the objectives of The Fund for Medi/Center 1; and in consideration of the commitments of others, I (we) hereby subscribe and agree to pay the total sum of $ _____

This commitment will be fulfilled in the following manner:

Paid herewith $ _____

The balance is to be paid in annual installments of
$ _____ commencing on _____ 19_____

Or, as follows: _____

And with the following provisions (if any): _____

Signature _____

Pledge reminders are to be mailed to: Name: _____

Address: _____

This gift opportunity presented by _____

All gifts are deductible for income tax purposes within the limits prescribed by law.

Checks should be made payable to:
"The Hospital of St. Raphael Expansion Program".

Securities should be endorsed in blank and sent by registered mail to:

Commitment and Response Expansion Program
The Hospital of St. R. . .
N.

In recognition of the vital function of The Hospital of St. Raphael in serving the health needs of the Greater New Haven Area, and in consideration of the gifts of others, I (we) hereby subscribe and agree to pay to THE HOSPITAL OF ST. RAPHAEL EXPANSION PROGRAM the sum of $ ....

Paid herewith: $ ....

The balance is to be paid in annual installments of
.... , 19 ......
commencing on ....

$

Or as follows: ....

.... Date ....

Signature ....

Statements are to   Name ....
be mailed to this address: Address ....

....

This gift opportunity presented by ....

all. Indeed, in addition to being clearly and logically organized with respect to their contents, subscription cards should be attractively designed, tastefully printed on good quality stock—sometimes almost in the form of a certificate—with artwork reflecting the institution's visual and/or graphic "identity."

11

Direct Mail

Direct mail is a well-known, widely used, and effective means of bringing a particular product, service, or appeal to the attention of large numbers of potential customers or donors at a low unit cost. Generally speaking, direct mail may be described as a "scatter shot" technique, at the opposite end of the scale from the in-person sales call or solicitation for philanthropic support.

Direct mail is playing a major and growing role in fund raising. For the right causes and under the right conditions, its use can tap large numbers of prospects productively and economically. Of course, considered *by itself*, the cost effectiveness of direct-mail fund raising cannot equal in-person solicitation and other techniques, but it is not intended to. Overall cost-effectiveness calculations, which include direct mail and other forms of solicitation, show that direct mail can be efficiently employed in numerous situations and, indeed, as techniques are refined, that direct mail will have greater application to increasing numbers of philanthropic institutions and causes.

Direct Mail in Fund Raising

Virtually all eleemosynary institutions have a need for direct mail in their fund-raising and development programs; for most, it is a continuous, if often unrecognized, need. Direct mail has wide application in annual giving programs, including alumni appeals, and can be used to enhance and extend the effectiveness of most capital campaigns, particularly in the wrap-up stages. The feedback provided by direct mail as potential larger donors are uncovered can be of great importance, as can direct mail's utility in measuring an organization's degree of visibility and credibility in the community, or among specific groups of prospects.

Volumes could be (and have been) written about the subject of direct mail as it applies to fund raising. This chapter will seek simply to present an overview of the science as it stands today, with comments on its application to some of the more common present fund-raising uses.

Direct mail, in this context, might be defined as the organized, systematic dissemination of mailed information about and appeals for support by a not-for-profit organization. Lists of names are assembled; letters, folders, pamphlets, brochures, and other printed materials are prepared; and mailings are made according to preplanned timetables. Each mailing typically includes a return vehicle for contributions.

Three factors are strikingly obvious about this technique. First, it can be no more effective than the quality of the lists and the accuracy with which they are compiled, used, and maintained. Second, the printed materials which carry the message must be carefully and imaginatively prepared. Third, to assure economic operation, and hence satisfactory cost-effectiveness ratios, the organization and management of a direct-mail program must be professionally planned and executed.

Components of a Direct-Mail Program
LISTS

Lists of names are available from two basic sources: the organization's own files, including files on alumni, friends, past donors, medical staff, employees, and so forth, and professional mailing list suppliers, which can furnish lists reflecting a wide variety of criteria to meet an individual institution's market profile. List selection and preparation is as much an art as a science and must reflect a thorough knowledge of the institution, its case, and its constituents.

PRINTED MATERIALS

Few individuals are heard to complain about a shortage of mail, especially "junk" mail, and, unfortunately, direct-mail appeals are often—and often deservedly—relegated to that category. They are much less likely to be, however, if the mailing vehicle is attractively designed and, while clearly identifying the name of the organization, is, if anything, understated. Then, assuming good list selection, the individual who receives an appeal from his or her alma mater, son or daughter's college, favorite symphony orchestra, local community hospital, firemen's fund, or United Way at least is instantly made aware of the pertinence to him of the message inside. Small, difficult-to-read return-address identification, in which the recipient may vaguely identify the word "hospital," "school," "appeal," or "fund," is an invitation to throw the mailing away. (Consistency in graphics for good recognition is important too, as every alumnus or alumna who receives an annual appeal can testify. If the college or university is *not* immediately recognizable from the copy, style, and design of the envelope, something is "wrong.")

Once the envelope is opened, the mailer unfolded, or the card turned over, the message *must* make its points swiftly, clearly, and emphatically. The personal approach is effective in many situations—a message over the signature of a classmate, president, known physician, prominent arts, political, sports figure, and so forth, or a statement "by" an individual (usually portrayed visually) whose appeal will be especially moving, such as an orphaned child or a blind person. Whenever possible, the solicitation letter copy should employ the "eye-to-eye" approach, writing as the individual would speak in person.

The space limitations inherent in most direct-mail materials can be turned to advantage if they are reflected in brevity, lucidity, and force in both the statement of the "case" and the definition of the action the reader is requested to take. For these reasons, the planning, writing, and design of direct-mail materials must obviously be carried out at a professional level. Bearing in mind the "competition in the mail-box," a frequent review of examples of direct mail from other organizations will often be productive.

Direct mail today is a highly developed fund-raising technique. Unfortunately, however, this does not prevent it from being applied inappropriately. It could be argued, indeed, that sporadic mailings, poor list selection, haphazard list maintenance, mediocre or uneven quality of printed materials, uncoordinated mailing schedules, poor or no use of follow-up mailings, and general amateurishness or incompetence can result in direct mail being not merely ineffective for a given organization or cause, but actually counterproductive. Certainly, to the extent that people heed a poorly planned and managed direct-mail program, it is likely that they will be impressed unfavorably—and that this impression will linger.

Primary Uses of Direct Mail in Fund Raising
ANNUAL APPEALS

Hospitals, colleges and universities, symphony orchestras, opera companies, ballet groups, museums and libraries, churches and religious groups, and various civic and social welfare organizations conduct annual mail appeals of a variety of kinds and sizes. Some, such as the United Way, Red Cross, and Easter Seal Society, are enormous, highly systematized and sophisticated nationwide operations with audiences in the millions; others are small, local efforts aimed at a few thousand individuals. The majority, perhaps, fall somewhere between these extremes. All seek one or more of three basic kinds of support: direct gifts, memberships, and "fulfillment" or premium gifts.

Most annual appeals operate on the assumption that the majority of individuals on the mailing lists know something about the organization (many of the names, of course, are persons who have supported it in the past), and the emphasis is typically on maximizing the *number* of relatively small recurrent gifts received. However, some annual appeals—most notably those run by college and university alumni associations—are tailored much more precisely to a sharply defined audience and, while seeking to maximize participation, also attempt to raise giving sights.

Annual appeal audiences can be divided into two major categories: individuals already acquainted with the organization or cause (and/or who have supported it in the past), and those who are being approached "cold," via purchased lists reflecting various economic and demographic considerations. In preparing the printed materials, this distinction should be kept in mind, although, practically speaking, there are limits to what can be accomplished in the average direct-mail flier or pamphlet in the way of presenting the organization's case in detail and depth.

ALUMNI APPEALS

These, as noted, are a specialized case in which an institution "talks" to a precisely defined audience which can be assumed to share common memories, experiences, and interests in the organization. Nevertheless, alumni direct-mail appeals must take certain factors into consideration:

1. *Alumni cannot be regarded as a homogeneous body.* An alumnus of the class of '19 and one of '79 may have very little in common other than the fact they attended the same institution (the institution, of course, typically will have changed enormously). Colleges and universities which have recently become coed usually find that the newer sex group's attitudes toward the institution differ in many ways from traditional attitudes. And, with changes in administration, curriculum, student mix, and so on, various schisms often develop among alumni. Because of these factors and the enormous value of having the individual alumnus be solicited by a classmate, the "class system" of organization is often followed in alumni fund appeals. Each class has agents, directed and coordinated by the alumni office, who, with other volunteers, directly contact their fellow classmates. The effectiveness of this approach, which for many institutions dates back more than half a century, has been well proved and documented.

2. *Alumni giving should, ideally, be made a recurring form of annual support of the donor's alma mater.* Of course, efforts should also be made to increase giving, but emphasis is rightly placed on

the importance of maintaining the highest possible percentage of participation. In other words, alumni giving becomes a "team" effort in which the rallying point may be the institution, a particular goal for alumni giving such as a new library or scholarship fund, the competitive spirit among various classes, and/or combinations of these.

3. *The role of alumni giving in inflationary times is particularly vital.* For many colleges and universities, annual giving provides a major portion of the income needed to bridge the widening gap between costs and income. Some colleges have employed the "living endowment" concept with conspicuous success among alumni, encouraging alumni to regard their gifts to the alumni fund as "replacing" the yield an endowment would generate if the institution had one. Direct mail is at the heart of such appeals, of course.

CAPITAL CAMPAIGNS

Direct mail has many applications in capital fund-raising programs. According to the principles of sequential fund raising, direct mail would usually emerge relatively near the bottom of the prospect list in terms of anticipated levels of giving. In other words, direct mail would be used to solicit relatively small gifts— but in relatively large numbers. However, it is possible that certain aspects or goals of a capital campaign might assign a higher giving level to certain direct-mail solicitations. For example, a medical center with a burn unit serving a large geographical area might use direct mail to solicit support for the burn unit as well as to approach direct-mail prospects for the campaign as a whole. The success of the Metropolitan Opera is an example of the use of direct mail on a nationwide basis to solicit support for a local organization which is nevertheless viewed by many as a national institution.

OTHER DEVELOPMENT EFFORTS

Direct mail can be used in a variety of other fund-raising efforts. Deferred giving programs are particularly suitable to direct mail since, as a rule, they are aimed at sharply defined constituencies, in the manner of alumni appeals. Many institutions use direct mail for specific one-shot projects or goals and as part of their general development program. The public relations implications of direct-mail campaigns, large and small, should always be kept in mind, as should the basic principles of effective institutional PR. Properly used, in addition to producing immediate revenue, direct mail can enhance, clarify, and heighten an organization's profile and image in a community. (This point underscores the importance of professional planning and management of all aspects of a direct-mail program, including preparation of printed materials.)

Setting Up A Direct-Mail Program

The ways and means by which a not-for-profit organization goes about setting up a direct-mail program will depend on a number of factors. In many cases, of course, direct-mail programs will already exist for one purpose or another, and, obviously, maximum advantage should be taken of existing capabilities. In a college or university, the alumni office often will have a direct-mail program in operation; if the development office decides to add direct mail, careful planning and close cooperation clearly will be essential.

Whether starting from scratch or revising or expanding an existing program, the following desiderata, among others, should guide the planning and thinking behind the development of a direct-mail fund-raising program.

1. Clear definitions of goals and purposes. These *must* be made in the context of the organization's master development plan. If no such plan exists, as a general rule an optimally productive direct-mail fund-raising program simply cannot be designed and implemented.

2. A review and analysis of available resources. In-house capabilities should be assessed carefully and realistically, in the context of defined goals and purposes.

3. Organization for direct mail. This entails determining who, specifically, will have responsibility for: (a) setting up and operating the program (including purpose, kind, frequency of mailings, follow-up mailings, and so forth), (b) meshing the program with

similar efforts under way, or contemplated, in such related areas as the alumni appeal, (c) making decisions about use of outside consultants, (d) periodically reviewing and evaluating the program's effectiveness, (e) hiring staff, (f) purchasing and/or leasing hardware, obtaining postage and stationery supplies, (g) establishing budgets, (h) list buying, file maintenance, record-keeping, and reporting, (i) preparing printed materials.

When the above questions have been thoroughly explored, and most of them answered, a basic outline for the direct-mail program, often best illustrated by a simple organization chart, can be prepared. In this process, serious advance consideration should be given to point (c), for fund-raising consultants very frequently can be of enormous assistance in the planning and start-up phases. Remember, like every other key component of a fund-raising program, the initial investment in establishing or revamping a direct-mail effort must be commensurate with real needs and requirements. Budgets should be created or found to ensure that the job is done right the first time. A direct-mail program that is not carefully thought out and implemented according to proven principles of management and operating procedure, far from producing needed revenues, can become a costly nightmare even in what may otherwise be an effective development operation.

Systematization

As noted in earlier chapters, accuracy is a cornerstone of effective fund-raising practice. This is particularly true in direct mail, in which large lists of names must be compiled, cross-checked, and maintained over long periods of time. As already noted, direct mail usually affects the organization's development effort directly and indirectly, producing immediate funds, preparing other individuals for later support, identifying individual and geographical sources of potential major support, presenting the organization's case and image to the public, and so forth. If this complex and critical operation is to have its maximum immediate and long-term effect, it must be built on a base of accurate management of the considerable amounts of information involved.

One way of looking at this information is by viewing it as consisting of answers to the following questions:

1. Who are the potential donors the program is seeking to reach?
2. What are their names, addresses, and telephone numbers?
3. What other information is known about them? Have they given before, and, if so, how much?
4. What further facts can be deduced from the foregoing?
5. Have they responded to previous mail appeals?
6. What, if anything, do the responses and known facts suggest about the individuals' potential for further support of the organization?
7. What other individuals and/or offices *in the organization* can make use of this information?
8. How can this information best be channeled to them?
9. By what means can lists of individuals recording this information best be kept up to date?
10. By what means can lists best be expanded, in accordance with the original goals and purposes of the program; new goals and purposes as these are identified; and changes or developments in the demographic factors on which the lists are based?
11. How can this information be stored safely for ready retrieval and updating?
12. What specific means should be used to transfer the information to (a) mailing labels, (b) acknowledgment forms, (c) recording and accounting forms, and (d) means of disseminating the information in accordance with question 7 above?

Considered in this way, the importance of systematization for direct mail becomes apparent. Various systems exist, of course, ranging from a simple box of 3×5 filing cards with names on addressograph plates to sophisticated card/tape computer systems with instantaneous printout, selective information retrieval/addition, and so forth, now available in the form of in-institution "mini terminals." The selection of a suitable system for a particular organization cannot be intelligently made until (1) a master operating plan for the direct-mail program has been established and (2) the questions above have been reviewed and answered in light of the institution's specific circumstances. The important subject of data processing is treated at length in the following chapter.

Direct Mail and Professional Counsel

The use of direct-mail consulting firms for fund raising has four major applications:

1. Consulting in the planning stages for a new or enhanced direct-mail program.
2. Consulting in the following start-up phase of the program, in which the steps described under "Systematization" usually take place.
3. Consulting in planning and preparation of specific direct-mail campaigns.
4. Creating and managing direct-mail programs and campaigns, on a periodic and/or continuous basis. This function usually includes providing appropriate hardware, purchasing lists, and the like.

Depending on the organization's in-house resources and the extent of the development office's experience and expertise, direct-mail professionals may advantageously be used for one or more of these applications. Broadly speaking, direct-mail service suppliers fall into two categories. First are direct-mail firms that manage complete direct-mail campaigns from initial consultations to buying or compiling the lists, preparing printed materials, making the mailings in the agreed-upon sequence, and so forth. For the client organization, such comprehensive services make it necessary, in fact, to do little more than receive, open, and record the contents of the return envelopes. Fees reflect the extent of the services contracted for. It can be assumed that reputable firms in this category have thorough basic knowledge, and usually wide experience, in direct-mail theory and practice, and will bring up-to-date technology and a generally high level of staff competence to bear.

The other source of professional direct-mail counsel is professional fund-raising firms, which are discussed at some length in Chapter 15. Many of these firms offer essentially the same services as the direct-mail houses, with the obvious advantage of thorough familiarity with the subject *from the fund-raising stand-point.* Such firms are more likely to take a holistic view of an organization's direct-mail needs and plans, in the context of its larger development and fund-raising situation (particularly if, as is often the case, they are working, or have worked, with the institution on a fund-raising study, capital campaign, or the like). Consequently, professional fund-raising firms are often much better qualified than direct-mail suppliers in the three direct-mail consulting functions described above and, in many cases, in the management function as well.

This is not to say that direct-mail suppliers do not regularly provide excellent service and produce satisfactory results. It is simply to point out that such firms do not, as a rule, have any specialized knowledge of fund raising per se, and that claims to the contrary should be taken with a grain of salt unless, or until, substantiated.

In selecting direct-mail counsel for fund raising, the criteria detailed in Chapter 15 should by all means be adhered to. Because lack of experience and/or in-house capability is the reason most not-for-profit organizations seek professional direct-mail assistance, it is particularly important to obtain the names of former clients from each firm under consideration and to check each reference carefully. How would the officer or institution evaluate the services received? Were the institution's objectives in hiring counsel met? Were the cost estimates accurate? Would the institution engage the same firm again for a similar program? A relatively small initial investment of time and trouble taken in checking the credentials of direct-mail counsel can pay sizable dividends in terms of the quality, suitability to the institution, and "staying-power" of its new or expanded direct-mail program.

12

Data Processing

The art of fund raising—to vastly oversimplify—could be said to consist of managing two kinds of information: the whereabouts of the money and the whereabouts of the leadership. Of course, obtaining this information and applying it intelligently are equally important; but there is no denying the primacy of the role played by the information itself. Consequently, every successful fund-raising professional qualifies for the popular new tag "information manager."

And indeed, the amounts of information to be managed are staggering and become more so every day. The names, addresses, occupations, giving history, and other pertinent facts about hundreds, and usually thousands, of individuals must be assembled and processed in practically every organized development and/or fund-raising effort. This information must be accurately gathered and maintained in some systematic fashion; it must be kept up to date; and it must be readily available for use by a number of departments and individuals.

Since every known method of fund raising has its basis for success in accurate, comprehensive, up-to-date, accessible records, it is not surprising that fund-raising professionals have, perhaps often without being aware of it, been in the forefront of developing new file maintenance and processing systems—in a word, data processing. Long before the advent of electronic data processing (EDP), fund raisers evolved their own methods, sometimes consisting of a simple "shoebox" card file, often sophis-

126

ticated and highly refined for list segmentation, coding, selectivity, and other data preparation and maintenance. The usual medium was file cards, with each entry made by hand. This required tedious attention to detail and was a repetitious, labor-intensive process which did not offer a way of processing (printing) directly from the source document.

Gradually, newer systems providing for some means of processing were developed and utilized, for example, the combination of a card with a stencil or plate (or even no card at all). The computer replaced many of these earlier maintenance and processing systems by card/tape systems, and later, disk/tape systems and terminal/tape systems, each offering the fund raiser greater control and management of his file of givers. The use of a terminal as a basic input device, with direct access to the computer, has reduced to some degree the dependence on card input, has aided and improved posting procedures, and has enhanced efficiency in access and updating of files.

Nevertheless, despite the degree of sophistication that has evolved over the years in computerization, many individuals and organizations continue to rely on their manual card systems, frequently for two good reasons. First, at the emotional and/or psychological levels, and because of concern about the often personal and/or confidential nature of their data, they simply are not about to part with this information, which is their lifeblood, in its most tangible and traditional form. Second, they are naturally hesitant about committing themselves to new systems and technologies which they do not completely understand and whose workings are not readily obvious. This chapter's thesis, however, is that the changeover from manual card files to card and/or other computer systems is long past due and represents a forward step which essentially is no different from the trailblazing efforts of earlier fund raisers in this area and which, once understood and correctly utilized, can yield important fund-raising benefits to numerous not-for-profit organizations.

Organization for Fund Raising

Data processing capabilities represent a management factor which every fund-raising professional must continually be aware of. The ramifications of an organization's data processing strengths (or weaknesses) extend to all areas of fund raising—direct-mail "marketing," ongoing development efforts, capital and other campaigns, annual (and alumni) giving, deferred giving programs, special events, and today's "thons." They simply cannot be ignored, treated as a mechanical process to be taken for granted, or seen as a low-priority matter for eventual review. Remember, what is at stake is nothing less than the accuracy, currency, and availability of the names of the individuals and groups that the organization relies upon for philanthropic support. A well-planned data processing system should, among other things, provide the organization with capabilities to:

- Store, retrieve, and select information accurately and efficiently.
- Organize various solicitations on the basis of factual analysis.
- Optimize productivity in all areas relating to information management, such as recording, reporting, receipting, acknowledging, and so forth.
  Improve fund-raising efficiency.

Elements of a Fund-Raising Data Processing System

An effective fund-raising data processing system should provide an organization with the following essential systems, which have application to most ongoing or planned development programs.

1. *Record System.* The system for recording and maintaining all information pertinent to an institution's fund-raising efforts.

   (a) A complete file of individual current donors, "lapses," "inactives," and others.
   (b) Information with respect to historical fact, including number and size of gifts over a given period, pledges, types of programs supported (annual, capital, membership, memorial, and so on), name/address, titles, relationship to the institution (alumnus, former patient, member, and so forth), zip, source of first contact, special codes

for processing selection/inhibiting and for packaging purposes.

(c) Numeric or alphanumeric coding (often referred to as "match codes") of each name for posting and updating the individual records on file.

(d) Information required to obtain or generate reports of giving activity (by number of gifts and by dollar amounts), statistical analysis, audit trails, and galley listings (which should replace maintaining duplicate in-office card listings).

2. *Processing System.* The system by which the information contained in the record system is managed and utilized for fundraising purposes.

(a) Ability to change sequence of files for printing purposes such as alpha and zip/alpha cheshire label mailings, for sequence and zip-code analysis, and for other reports.

(b) Addressing capabilities, from basic cheshire label mailing programs to computer letters.

(c) Capabilities which permit the selection and inhibiting of certain types of donors from one or all printouts and/or mailings.

(d) Packaging capabilities whereby the computer assigns to every individual on file a key code which designates the specific type of handling and appeal package an individual would receive for mailings and other purposes.

(e) Tape-to-tape merge/purge, "dupe" elimination, net naming capacity. The system's capacity for selecting and editing tapes enables an organization to compare an outside tape of names/records with the house list to effect a net name result (that is, a list without duplications) for cold prospect mailings.

(f) Computer printing capability at high speeds, with upper and lower case, and for computer letters and reports.

3. *Production and Mailing System.* Production of appeal package materials and the mailing program are natural extensions of the record and processing systems, although not always seen that way, and lead simultaneously into a closely related "specialty"

area—direct mail. Essentially, two steps are involved: planning and preparation of materials—folders, cards, brochures, and so on—and the utilization of these in a direct-mail program. The subject of direct mail is covered in Chapter 11.

Converting to EDP

As suggested earlier, the decision to take this important step is not always made wholly on a rational basis. The sense of security which existing (but often outmoded) systems give, fear of a new technology, worries about actually losing critical information, all play a part. Equally a factor, it might be suggested, is laziness.

Certainly no organization should make the decision to go to EDP lightly. A thorough and searching review first must be undertaken of the institution's present and future development and fund-raising plans as well as of its present data processing capabilities. Ideally, this process should be integrated into an institutionwide appraisal of data processing needs and resources. Frequently an organization will fail to take advantage of existing EDP capabilities simply because of poor interdepartmental communications (and the lack of a careful definition of development needs, as noted). It is not uncommon, for example, to discover that a major university's, hospital's, or other agency's advanced and sophisticated computer capabilities are not used at all by some departments, such as the development and alumni offices. Obviously, computer link-ups are not magically going to sprout in these offices, and the initiative will usually have to come from the departments concerned. Indeed, the development office may have to "fight" for computer access, because, typically, its needs—or potential as a "computer customer"—were not considered when the organization installed the computer in the first place. The lesson here is: the development office must analyze and quantify its data processing needs and make these known to the administration.

In many instances, of course, development/fund-raising computer needs will ultimately be found to be best served from outside the institution. The review process necessary to determine the extent to which the organization's development/fund-raising arm can benefit from EDP to some degree actually comprises a model for the "ideal" data processing system for the organization at a given time and would include, among others, these key steps and checkpoints:

1. Definitions
   (a) Systems description (even if plugging into another system).
   (b) Complete documentation of all systems; software checked (programs debugged).
   (c) Processing cycle established and schedule drawn up for all EDP and associated work.
   (d) Determination made of use of batch processing (if desirable).
   (e) Arrangements made for security of all computer files and programs (duplicate, up-to-date copy of records stored off premises).
2. Housecleaning Procedures
   (a) Apply all changes of address, historical, and other data to individual files.
   (b) Redo all individual files which are not legible for conversion purposes.
   (c) Carry out any additional pre-coding.
3. Input stage (prior to conversion)
   (a) Analysis and definition of method of conversion—keypunch, type-scanning, key-disk, or direct terminal.
   (b) Determination of whether conversion will be in-house or out-of-house.
   (c) Timing and schedules established.
   (d) Verification procedure established for checking converted data. (The first three methods cited in (a) above have an error factor which must be considered; the direct-terminal method should be almost error-free.)
   (e) Selection of type of account number for every record.
4. Output stage (after conversion)
   (a) Galley listing of converted names/addresses/records.
   (b) Galley reviewed and approved by director of development, alumni affairs, or the like. All corrections and additions to be made on galley, which is then returned for computer updating.
   (c) Updated galley listing is furnished to the institution,

replacing the former card file or other systems records. Each time the file is updated, a new updated galley should be provided (for "white mail" lookup).
(d) Ready-to-produce status checked for:
Cheshire labels.
Pressure-sensitive labels.
Statistical reports.
Computer letters.
Merge/purge activity.
Other.

The considerable amount of information the foregoing analysis and review process should produce will need to be organized and converted into a written report. It is on the basis of this report that the decision whether, when, and to what kind of EDP system the existing system should be converted can then be made. There are several important points to keep in mind at this stage:

1. The information elicited from the data processing analysis and review should be studied carefully in the context of present and planned development/fund-raising programs and, ideally, in light of the organization's master development plan (see Chapter 2).

2. The conversion to EDP per se is a technical change, like the conversion of a heating system from coal to oil. The end result—by which the process should be judged—should be equal or superior to results from the system previously in use, in terms of accuracy, currency, speed, accessibility, or combinations of these, and usually should yield improved cost-effectiveness benefits, although these are difficult to quantify and cannot always be expected at once. In short, the basic *information management function* served by the previous data processing system should be enhanced, but not necessarily altered.

3. The first step in converting to EDP is the major and most critical one. It should be taken only upon careful consideration of the factors noted above, and other pertinent information. Once the basic conversion decision has been made, it should allow for the accommodation of more foreseeable areas of future need. An EDP system which "will serve for a few years" is not worth converting to, although it should be borne in mind that at the present rate of developments in this fast-moving area, basic im-

provements and upgrading can be expected on a fairly frequent basis.

4. The well-known adage "GI-GO" ("garbage in, garbage out") applies equally to the use of computer technology (and, in fact, to any data processing system), and to the actual decision-making process leading to conversion.

5. While the decision to convert to EDP should certainly take account of the number of names on file, there is no magic point above which EDP is warranted and below which it is not. Much more valuable criteria are the degrees of productivity, effectiveness, and utilization that EDP capabilities can be expected to confer. Productivity and effectiveness, of course, are related directly to operating costs and, consequently, to income development. The potential for increased utilization of the data processing system may allow for the development of ancillary fund-raising activities capable of sufficiently increasing overall philanthropic income to offset some EDP operating costs. For example, the capacity at a given institution to establish a new, potentially productive deferred giving, direct-mail program, utilizing new or planned EDP capabilities, should be considered in the decision-making review process regarding conversion to a computer data processing system.

The Role of Professional Counsel

The decision to convert (or not to convert) to EDP is a critical one for an organization's development office; it therefore makes sense, in addition to conducting a thorough internal audit of data processing needs and capabilities, to consider the role professional counsel can play. Generally speaking, there are three chief areas in which counsel is most effective:

1. Consulting with respect to the decision to convert to EDP. This includes reviewing the foregoing considerations in the context of the organization's development and fund-raising plans and needs and relating these to existing EDP systems. From such consulting should come specific recommendations regarding planning, timing, choice of kind of EDP system, in-house versus out-of-house capability, and so forth. Ideally, such counseling will take into consideration the client institution's EDP capability as a

whole, although, for the reasons already given, it is not always practical or even desirable to integrate development and fund-raising EDP capabilities with the institution's other computer functions.

2. Consulting with respect to planning specific EDP programs, once the conversion to the computer has been made. This counseling in effect is concerned with helping the organization maximize its new EDP potential in all aspects of development and fund raising. For example, the application of EDP to annual giving or the alumni fund will often benefit from professional counsel in the planning and start-up phases.

3. Managing EDP programs and services. Depending on the organization's needs and its staffing resources, it is often productive to assign the management of specific EDP-related programs, in whole or in part, to professional counsel. For example, a community hospital decides to establish an annual giving program using direct mail, but lacks in-house capability to plan and implement such a program. On review, it is determined that the use of professional counsel should yield greater productivity and cost effectiveness than attempting to do the job in-house. Similarly, institutions with extensive EDP resources and experience may decide that for a given program, professional counsel is likely to be able to do a better job, more quickly, at lower cost.

Selecting EDP Counsel

There are two broad sources of data processing counsel for not-for-profit institutions: (1) data processing/EDP vendors and service bureaus and (2) professional fund-raising firms. The former typically specialize in EDP services (often including direct mail) for a wide variety of applications; the latter approach EDP first from the special perspective of *fund-raising and development needs,* and also provide experience and expertise in EDP services for direct-mail programs. Obviously, other things being equal, this perspective is a valuable one, likely to result in services and programs more sensitively attuned to the real needs the institution seeks to address.

Professional fund-raising counsel offering EDP services also almost always provides a full range of fund-raising services—consulting, conducting studies, providing campaign management, and offering ancillary services. Hence, it is in the position of a specialist who is able to approach EDP applications from the broader vantage point of institutional development. This is not to say, of course, that using professional fund-raising counsel for EDP consulting and management is in every case best for a given institution. There are many variables at work. Sometimes when professional fund-raising counsel has been retained to plan, implement, and manage an EDP system, it may recommend the use of a large "house" for a particular program.

The satisfactory choice of professional counsel for EDP services depends on two primary factors: matching the capabilities of counsel to the real needs of the development or other fund-raising department; and evaluating the capabilities of firms being considered. Both aspects of this task must be given the time and attention necessary to ensure a satisfactory outcome. The general comments about the selection of professional fund-raising counsel in Chapter 15 apply with equal force to the selection of counsel for EDP services.

13

Deferred Gifts and Bequests

Simply stated, a deferred gift is a present commitment that will financially benefit an eleemosynary organization at a later date. This commitment may take the form of a trust arrangement which pays the donor lifetime income and offers tax benefits, a bequest in his or her will, or a gift of life insurance.

For numerous institutions, deferred giving is an increasingly important source of immediate and potential income. In addition to the dollar value of such support, deferred giving helps an institution plan realistically for its financial future, and can assist it in attracting increased philanthropic support by telling it who its friends are.

For donors, deferred giving also has important advantages. It enables individuals who might otherwise not be able to make a gift at all to support organizations and causes of their choice. It frequently makes it possible for them to make larger gifts. And deferred giving can confer significant tax benefits, which often make this form of giving even more attractive.

This chapter will describe the more common forms of deferred giving and some of the ways such programs are typically conducted by not-for-profit institutions. The information, current as of 1980, has general applicability to large and small institutions, to organizations seeking to enhance the effectiveness and scope of their deferred giving programs, and to those planning to establish such a program for the first time.

Components of a Deferred Giving Program
RETAINED LIFE INCOME GIFTS

A retained life income gift is a gift which pays lifetime income to the donor or others before it is to be used by a charitable institution. Individual X, for example, decides he can give $10,000 in securities to institution Y if he can continue to receive income from the gift under a life income plan. He is pleased to find that his gift also entitles him to important tax benefits. An immediate income tax deduction may be claimed, a capital gains tax on the appreciated portion of the $10,000 is avoided, and the entire amount of the gift will be removed from his estate, resulting in estate tax savings. X can choose from four options. Each will pay lifetime income to him (and a survivor, if he chooses), and each offers immediate and long-term benefits.

1. *Charitable remainder unitrust.* A unitrust is a *separate trust* established by transferring cash, securities, or other property to a trustee (a bank or directly to the institution, which acts as trustee). Each year the trustee pays to the beneficiary or beneficiaries a fixed percentage of the trust's annual value. The percentage, established by the donor, must be 5 percent or more in order to qualify for the deductibility under federal tax law. Lifetime income can be paid to the donor or others—for example to the donor for life, and then to his spouse if she survives him.

The income tax deduction—available immediately—is based on government tables which take into consideration the percentage to be paid and the ages of the income beneficiaries. There is no capital gains tax to be paid on donated property which has appreciated, and the property is removed from the donor's estate for estate tax purposes.

EXAMPLE ■ Mr. A., age 65, holds $50,000 of appreciated common stock which has been paying 4 percent in dividends over the years. He decides he can make a gift to his alma mater if he does not have to sacrifice the income he had been earning from the stock. He transfers the securities to his bank as trustee and specifies that 6 percent of the annual value of the trust be paid to him for life and then to his wife, age 63, if she survives him. The trust is then to be transferred to his college to establish a scholarship fund. In the year of the gift, $15,882 of the $50,000 gift is available for income tax deduction purposes; he avoids paying a capital gains tax on the appreciated portion of the donated securities; and the entire gift will be removed from his taxable income, reducing his estate tax. Although the 6 percent payment is constant, actual income will vary if the value of the trust varies. All things being equal, however, his income will probably increase as a result of having created the trust.

2. *Charitable remainder annuity trust.* An annuity trust is similar to a unitrust except that a fixed dollar amount, rather than a percentage, is paid to the donor (and then to another beneficiary, if so arranged). This payment will not fluctuate but remains constant throughout the life of the trust. According to law, the annual payment must be at least 5 percent of the value of the property at the time it is transferred to the trust. Again, an immediate income tax deduction is available and is determined by the income to be paid and the age of the income beneficiary or beneficiaries. Appreciated property creating the trust escapes capital gains taxation and is removed from the donor's estate, providing estate tax relief.

EXAMPLE ■ Mrs. B., a 70-year-old widow, has $50,000 of common stock which is worth a great deal more than it was when acquired by her late husband. She would like to create a memorial in his name at her local hospital but needs the income the securities generate—some 3 percent annually. Further, she is concerned about the future and would like to increase rather than decrease her income. To meet her two objectives, Mrs. B. creates a charitable remainder annuity trust at her bank. The trust is to pay her $2,500 (5 percent of the $50,000 gift) annually for the rest of her life, and then the amount of the trust is to be transferred to the hospital to create the memorial. Immediately, $30,192 is available for a charitable deduction on Mrs. B.'s tax return, no capital gains tax is due, and estate tax savings will result. Mrs. B. receives satisfaction in knowing she has made a meaningful gift in her husband's memory, and the hospital can count on future support.

3. *Charitable gift annuity.* The gift annuity contains many features of the annuity trust but differs in one main respect. In the annuity trust, the dollar figure to be paid is set by the donor; in the case of the gift annuity, the amount to be paid is determined by the ages of the income beneficiaries. The higher the ages, the higher the rate. Gift annuity rates are established by the Commit-

tee on Gift Annuities, a nonprofit organization formed to recommend rates, the form of contract, and so on. Most charitable institutions offering gift annuities follow the rates recommended by the committee.

Another difference is the tax treatment of appreciated property. Establishing a unitrust or annuity trust avoids capital gains taxation; with a gift annuity, there may be some capital gains tax to be paid, depending on the particular situation.

EXAMPLE ■ Miss C, age 60, with no heirs, would like to support a national social service organization for which she volunteers time. She has no stocks or bonds, but does have a sizable amount in a bank savings account which earns 5 percent interest. She establishes a $5,000 gift annuity with the organization and specifies that at her death, her gift be used to purchase equipment. In the meantime, Miss C. will receive $290 (5.8 percent) per year and is entitled to an immediate income tax deduction of $1,407 for having made the gift. Miss C. is pleased to know that she is making a larger gift than would be possible were it not deferred. Further, she increases her income slightly and receives tax benefits for having made the gift.

4. *Life income agreement.* A life income agreement is a gift of cash, securities, or other property to a fund consisting of other life income gifts. The donor (or the donor and another income beneficiary, if so arranged) will receive a lifetime income, which depends on the annual income from the fund. The fund can be maintained by the institution, or for the institution by a bank or trust company. An immediate charitable gift deduction is available, which takes into account the number of beneficiaries, their age and sex, and the fund's earning history. No capital gains tax is paid on appreciated property used to create a gift, and the full amount of the gift is excluded from the donor's estate for tax purposes.

EXAMPLE ■ Mr. D, age 58, has securities which cost him $15,000 and now have a market value of $25,000. He gives the securities to a life income fund operated by a foundation which supports his church. Each year, on a quarterly basis, Mr. D. receives his proportionate share of the fund's income, and Mrs. D, also age 58, will continue to receive income payments for life if she outlives her husband. The fund has been earning 7 percent, and this plus the ages of Mr. and Mrs. D. entitle them to a contribution deduction of $5,375. There is no capital gains tax on the $10,000 appreciation, and the entire value of the gift will be removed from Mr. D.'s estate at his death.

GIFTS OF LIFE INSURANCE

Many individuals own life insurance policies originally purchased to meet needs that no longer exist. They may have acquired insurance to protect young children now grown and on their own, or to safeguard a struggling family business which is now flourishing. These policies can be given to nonprofit institutions in several ways. One, the institution can be named as beneficiary of an existing policy. This will aid the organization in the future and give the donor eventual tax relief. Two, the donor can make the institution owner and beneficiary of the policy. Since the donor has relinquished control of the policy, he receives an immediate tax deduction approximating its cash surrender value. Further, if the donor continues to pay the premiums on the assigned policy, he may deduct these payments each year as a charitable contribution. Three, the donor can purchase a new policy naming the institution as owner and beneficiary, and continue to pay the premiums on it. The premium payments are deductible, and the proceeds will not be subject to federal estate taxation.

EXAMPLE ■ Mr. E. owns a $40,000 whole life policy which was purchased when his only child was born. The present value of the policy is $20,000, and the annual premium is $1,600. His daughter is married, with a career of her own, and the policy's protection is no longer necessary. Mr. E., therefore, names his church as owner and beneficiary and continues to pay the annual premiums. He receives three benefits: the $20,000 present value of the policy is deductible as an immediate income tax contribution, the $1,600 annual premiums will now be deductible, and the full $40,000 face falue of the policy will be removed from Mr. E.'s taxable estate.

GIFTS OF HOME WITH RETAINED LIFE OCCUPANCY

Through this plan, it is possible to deed one's home to an institution while continuing to live in it for life (it will not become the property of the institution until the death of the survivor). For making this transfer, the donor is entitled to an immediate income tax deduction which depends on his age (and that of any other life beneficiary) and the value of the home.

EXAMPLE ■   Mr. F., age 64, is contemplating retirement and is in the process of rewriting his will. He has decided that his alma mater should receive his home after he and his wife, age 63, are no longer living. Their children are to be provided for in other ways. Mr. F. learns that he can receive an immediate benefit if, instead of making the transfer by will, he deeds his home to his college and continues to reside in the house for as long as he and his wife live. The house and property have a fair market value of $125,000. This, the ages of Mr. and Mrs. F., and other factors allow an immediate charitable deduction of some $52,000. Hence three important benefits are available to Mr. and Mrs. F.: the ability to continue to live in their house as before, an immediate tax deduction, and the satisfaction of knowing that Mr. F.'s college will benefit in the future.

BEQUESTS

By far the most popular and well-known deferred giving option is the bequest, defined as a direction in a will to distribute personal property. Income from bequests is especially important to many not-for-profit organizations. In fact, for some such institutions bequests are the largest single source of support. Apart from the personal satisfaction the donor has of knowing an institution of his or her choice will benefit in the future, a gift by bequest offers estate tax advantages, being fully deductible from one's estate and often placing the resultant taxable estate in a lower tax bracket.

Philanthropic organizations can be named in one's will in a number of ways. An *outright bequest* specifies that funds or property be transferred directly to the institution. A *remainder interest* assigns the "remainder" after specific sums have been disbursed to other beneficiaries. Finally, a *contingent bequest* provides for distribution to an institution only if one or more named beneficiaries do not survive the individual creating the bequest.

EXAMPLE ■   Mr. G., a bachelor, has an adjusted gross estate of

$300,000. He could leave his estate to his nephew (a successful businessman) and would have an estate tax of $40,800.* Instead, his will gives a total of $200,000 to be divided among several philanthropic institutions, and the other $100,000 to his nephew. As a result of the $200,000 charitable deduction, Mr. G.'s estate tax is reduced to zero, saving the estate $40,800 in estate taxes.

The All-Too-Typical Deferred Giving Program— Or Nonprogram

With a few notable exceptions, deferred giving has long been the "poor relation" in nonprofit institutional development efforts. Typical "programs," indeed, often consist of nothing more than an occasional appeal to the organization's constituents to include the institution in their wills. Some institutions attempt more systematically to promote bequests, gifts of life insurance, and perhaps the separate life income trusts—all forms of deferred giving that do not require the organization to deal directly with the donor. A small number of charitable institutions establish pooled income funds of their own and actively promote all components of a deferred giving program.

The primary reason that deferred giving is given such cursory treatment by so many not-for-profit institutions is the familiar one of manpower shortage. The development office typically lacks the staff, time, and, in many cases, the expertise to establish and operate an effective deferred giving program. Many organizations, while acknowledging the potential value of deferred giving, tend to relegate it to a relatively low-priority, "some day" goal, perhaps partly because, by its very nature, deferred giving does not usually produce immediate income.

Establishing a Deferred Giving Program

Obviously, a "back burner" approach to deferred giving can be very costly to an institution in terms of lost support—some of which, indeed, will undoubtedly go to other organizations with

---

* This assumes Mr. G. dies after 1981, the date the full unified transfer tax credit takes effect.

more active deferred giving programs. The primary requirement for success in this area of fund raising is the real desire to raise "future money," based on an understanding of what this can mean to the institution.

Although this may appear obvious, what is equally or more obvious is that many institutions—understandably—prefer to concentrate primarily or solely on seeking immediate, outright contributions. Yet, as explained in Chapter 2, the master development plan, which is an essential part of every charitable institution's short- and long-term fund-raising efforts, must consider each and every source of support, establishing realistic goals and priorities in light of the organization's needs and resources. In the case of deferred giving, it is true that the resources often have to be "created," and this should be done, in most cases, with the blessing (and promise of support) of the governing board. The trustees should be told exactly what is proposed, when results may be expected, and what the board's role will be.

Planning must be done carefully to ensure that the deferred giving effort dovetails realistically and efficiently with other development programs. The individuals in charge of creating the program should put the plan in writing and make certain that all those involved—board members, administrators, volunteers—understand it, approve of it, and intend to back it. It is essential that those who make decisions for the institution recognize that in most cases deferred gifts will not provide *actual income* for a number of years but that, obviously, the sooner the organization is in a position to actively encourage deferred giving, the sooner income from this source can be realized.

Encouraging Deferred Gifts

Rarely does a person begin the day saying, "This morning, after breakfast, I am going to create a charitable remainder unitrust." To bring an individual to this point, he or she must first be told what a unitrust (or other deferred gift) is and how it would benefit the donor as well as the institution receiving it, and in fact specifically be asked to consider making such a gift.

Although deferred giving can be promoted in a variety of ways—simple bequest reminders, direct-mail advertisements, newsletter articles, word of mouth, volunteers contacting prospects directly, and so forth—the most effective method in most cases unquestionably is the direct, one-on-one approach. Nothing is better than to have a volunteer contact a prospect and say, "Joe, I'm involved in the deferred giving program for our hospital (or preparatory school, university, symphony orchestra, church, museum, or whatever), and I think one of the plans we have might just work for you. Let's have lunch next week and find out." Of course, such efforts can be made only once a basic deferred giving plan has been approved and put into operation. The procedural rules for operating such a program generally follow those given in Chapter 5 with respect to such important factors as leadership identification and enlistment, prospect research and rating, and so forth.

Outside Assistance

While not every institution can or even should set up a full in-house deferred giving program, every not-for-profit organization's board, administration, and development office should have at least basic familiarity with the subject, and the majority can expect to benefit from a deferred giving program realistically tailored to the institution's development goals, resources, and constituencies for potential support. Professional associations, such as the Council for Advancement and Support of Education (CASE), can be an excellent source of assistance for organizations able to benefit from the special conferences and training aids offered to members.

An effective means of assessing an organization's deferred giving potential and determining what kind of program would be best is to hire professional fund-raising counsel. Many firms and some individuals offer specialized consulting and management services in specific areas such as deferred giving. An institution with a large development department may require only initial or periodic assistance, while one with a one-man development office may be in a position to benefit from full-time assistance. The subject of professional fund-raising firms and counsel is treated in Chapter 15, and most of the points covered apply directly to institutions planning to establish a deferred giving program or seeking to enhance an existing one.

14

Federal Grantsmanship

As noted earlier in these pages, the federal government can be an important source of funding for many not-for-profit organizations. Government grantsmanship, a somewhat specialized branch of fund raising, requires the successful application of basic procedures and techniques which have many similarities to—and some important differences from—private-sector fund raising. This chapter will present an overview of the subject, with some specific comments about key topics including project development, proposal writing, "packaging" and "marketing" the proposal, and managing a federal grants program—a function analogous to, and frequently part of, the organization's regular development program.

Grant Opportunities

At the present time there are numerous programs of various kinds allocating federal dollars to philanthropic agencies. These funding programs are established through Congressional action and are implemented by one of the executive departments, making monies available for individual or organizational research projects, institutional support, demonstration projects, student aid, and so on.

The legislation authorizing each one of the grant opportunities also designates the agency in charge. However, the appropriations process is a separate legislative act, and it is quite possible for an existing or proposed program not to get funded or to be funded below the authorized level. The *Catalog of Federal Domestic Assistance,* issued annually by the Office of Management and Budget, is a compendium of all federal programs which provide assistance, grants, and benefits. This is an essential tool for all persons working in the federal grants field. Also important is the *Federal Register,* and there are many other publications of various agencies which can be very useful in an organization's efforts to secure federal grant dollars.

Because of definition disagreements and the difficulty of obtaining uniform data on all types of funding from the multitude of federal entities, there is no accurate assessment of total grants dollars available. Suffice it to say that there are several billions up for grabs.

Seeking Federal Dollars

In many respects, the process for obtaining federal grants is quite similar to that of soliciting major gifts from corporations or private foundations. Regardless of the prospective funding source, the process begins with the formulation of an idea, continues through project development, and concludes with proposal preparation, identification of possible funding sources, packaging and marketing the proposal, and—assuming success—administering the grant.

PROJECT DEVELOPMENT

Regardless of whether the support target is an individual, a private foundation, or the federal government, the development of a project which will require outside funding is exactly the same. This statement assumes, of course, that the compelling factor is the project's real importance to the organization's overall program, not merely the availability of funds. This is an important point, because all too often federal funds have been solicited seemingly because of their availability and not because the particular project complemented the prospective grantee's mission. When temptations to follow such a course are not resisted, program disjointment and financial disarray almost invariably quickly follow.

A project emanates usually from the mind of one or more persons to satisfy a particular need. A brief description of the project, its purposes, benefits, and rough financial implications should be prepared for internal review and approval. Each organization should have a specifically prescribed procedure to follow in the evolution of a project from concept to formal application for funding, to assure conformity with organizational purposes, policies, and budgetary restraints. Ultimately, the chief executive officer is responsible for adherence to such specified procedures, but usually an officer at least one level lower is delegated to enforce the rules.

COMPONENTS OF A PROPOSAL

Each proposal should contain at least 10 major components:

1. An abstract, or summary statement.
2. A statement of the problem or questions to be addressed.
3. The goals or purposes of the project.
4. Measurable objectives or expected quantitative outcomes.
5. Procedures and a calendar to be followed to achieve the objectives.
6. An evaluative assessment, or built-in evaluation tools.
7. Multiplier factors, or uses to which the findings can be put for a broader segment of the population.
8. Descriptions of facilities and equipment necessary.
9. Availability of qualified personnel, and their designation.
10. A detailed budget.

Each proposal should also contain a covering title sheet, a table of contents, and appendixes of material which supports any portion of the body of the proposal. In addition, details such as full names, titles, addresses, and rank (if applicable) should be included along with the signed approval of the officer given that authority by the organization.

PROPOSAL PREPARATION

A proposal usually will go through several drafts, and should receive critical examination by several knowledgeable people. Every effort must be made to develop as clear and concise a statement as possible. If the project idea hasn't been formulated sufficiently or suffers from fuzzy, undisciplined thinking, the proposal will almost always reflect this need for further work.

Most federal funding agencies have guidelines for the grant opportunities within their purview. These guidelines, and any suggested proposal format, should be adhered to, and the final product should be neat, simply packaged, and organized and submitted according to directives. Jargon and "buzzwords" should be avoided; too often they signal failure to achieve clarity in the planning stage. Finally, of course, the proposal should be carefully edited to ensure it embodies that classic trio of desirable qualities for such a document—lucidity, ease, and force.

SOURCES OF SUPPORT

Selection of a funding source ideally should come before the proposal is first prepared in draft form. Although the information sought is generally the same, funding sources, as already noted, vary in their guidelines and suggested formats for proposals. After approval of the project for funding application, an abstract or preliminary proposal should be prepared. The *Catalog of Federal Domestic Assistance* is an initial source for identifying agencies which might be interested in funding the project. The grants office files will—or should—have material describing most funding opportunities from federal sources. The criteria should be read carefully to make sure that the project, organization, and purposes meet the stated requirements.

PACKAGING AND MARKETING THE PROPOSAL

Now that a project has had internal approval and support sources have been identified, the tough job of getting it funded begins. Some people refer to this process as "packaging" and "marketing" a proposal, but by whatever name it's called, it involves working with the internal project director or team, and often with federal agency personnel.

If, after careful reading of the purposes, criteria, and application procedures of federal grant programs, more than one potential funding source appears feasible, letters of inquiry should be written to each source. (Most federal programs are so carefully constructed, or were enacted to meet such specific purposes, that multiple funding source possibilities will be rare.) Since program officers in most cases are people who sincerely try to get the best proposals for consideration by their agency, a letter or a personal visit can be of great help in the final preparation of the proposal. However, although agency officers are willing to help in ways such as interpreting guidelines and clarifying questions, they are not there to write proposals. Their time should not be abused prior to the submission of a proposal, nor should they be hounded for progress information after submission.

For the purposes of the letter of inquiry, either the abstract or an expanded two-page description of the project may be used. The funding proposal, as suggested earlier, should be prepared in a simple, clear format, in which full compliance with the agency's specifications is one of the most important ingredients. Often organizations are tempted, when presenting a funding proposal, to enlist the aid of a congressman or senator, or one of their representatives. Resist this temptation; any semblance of pressure can be a tactical mistake, although it certainly does no harm for an institution to inform its local congressman that the proposal has been submitted.

One final comment regarding packaging and marketing the proposal: It's all for naught if the submission deadline isn't met!

GRANTS ADMINISTRATION

Although this chapter essentially is concerned with project development and proposal preparation, a few comments on grants administration are not out of place. Too often institutions and organizations forget the all-important follow-through to assure that a project is accomplished once a grant is made. Special budgetary, accounting, and auditing procedures should be in place to administer all grants, particularly federal ones. Without them, an organization is flirting with danger, as failure to properly administer a grant not only will adversely affect the program it was obtained for, but can harm the organization's future efforts to obtain federal grants and to attract private philanthropic support.

Private Sources and the Federal Grants Process— Some Differences

Although, as noted, many similarities exist between federal grants acquisition and solicitation of corporations and private foundations, there also are important differences. Numerous federal grants programs emanate directly from legislation, and all are bound by strict federal procedures and Congressional review. The agencies which administer such grants, therefore, must operate for the public interest and in the public eye, and tend, on the whole, to stress specific criteria and guidelines more than their funding counterparts in the private sector. In a further effort to ensure openness in the grant-making process, and also to recruit experienced personnel, many federal agencies employ peer-review panels to screen and evaluate proposals, which makes it all the more important that every procedural "i" has been dotted and "t" crossed throughout the project development and proposal preparation stages.

A final important difference in working with federal agencies is that a much longer period is usually required from the time of the deadline for proposal and submission to the awards announcement. (This is not absolutely true in all instances, but one should be prepared for it.) Much of the delay results from the quantity of proposals which have to be processed, but some is endemic in the system.

Managing a Federal Grants Program

Managing a federal grants program is not unlike directing a development effort for private gifts, with the difference that there is only one prospect. In many organizations, the private-fund development director also oversees federal grants applications. In others, particularly large private and public universities, there is an office separate from the development office handling research and sponsored programs.

Obviously, coordination is not a severe problem with one person handling both areas, but it does become an important factor with multiple individuals and offices involved. In the latter situation, indeed, there must be strict coordination in both the selection of projects and the determination of funding sources. Because many projects could possibly qualify for funding from either private foundations or the federal government, the chief grants officer and the development director must work closely together. In cases when a multiple solicitation is determined to be advisable, this operation must be carefully orchestrated. Discipline must also be maintained by the chief executive officer, or his designated deputy, over the project development and approval process.

A question affecting many organizations in the management of a federal grants program is how best to deal with the geographical problems of distance from Washington. Some institutions have one or several staff persons available to commute when necessary to see agency personnel face to face. Others establish a Washington office, while still others retain specialized counsel. However, it is difficult to cite clear-cut guidelines, based on federal grant activity, for establishing a Washington office or committing a person full time to the effort. The actual volume of federal grants sought by a given institution does not seem to be a consistent criterion.

From a management perspective, one person can certainly oversee both functions—private fund raising and federal grants acquisition—and perhaps this is the most useful ground rule that can be formulated. However, in most cases, if an institution is serious about attempting to raise major sums of money from either sector, it probably should not combine the functions within the job description of one individual, since both functions are sufficiently involved to require the attention of at least one person full time.

So, if there is a question of either/or—in other words, if only one person is available or can be financed—then the organization has to make an initial assessment of whether its greatest potential is in the private or public sector. (This criterion, if objectively applied, would be valid not only for determination of the job description of the first person employed, but for all others that follow to accommodate growth.)

A final significant difference between federal and private solicitation is the role of volunteerism and the use of volunteers. Few if any volunteers become part of the solicitation process for federal grants, while it is usually hoped that many volunteers will become part of private-sector efforts. For these reasons, while it is important that the person who directs private-sector fund raising understand and be imbued with volunteerism, this quality is much less important in seeking grants from the federal government, and hence the job qualifications for these two development positions diverge in this and other ways, perhaps affording organizations greater latitude in selection of a director and staff for its federal grants acquisition program.

15

Professional Firms

Institutional fund-raising efforts have, on the whole, kept pace with the steady increases in total philanthropic giving in the past quarter century. It is in fact a moot point whether increased total giving has resulted from, among other things, intensified fund-raising efforts or whether the availability of more gift billions has necessitated increasingly professional approaches to fund raising. One thing is certain: a major factor in the ability of the nation's not-for-profit agencies, foundations, institutions, and other organizations to expand and heighten the effectiveness of their development efforts has been the availability of professional fund-raising counsel, which has had a particularly significant impact on improving fund-raising cost effectiveness. For the purposes of this discussion, we shall define professional counsel as fund-raising firms and individual consultants specializing in assisting not-for-profit institutions in their development efforts.

What Professional Counsel Does

A basic definition can perhaps best be given as follows: the role of professional counsel is not to raise money, but *to help the institution raise it*. Reputable counseling firms do not guarantee results or raise money directly—that is, their staff do *not* solicit or promise to raise unattainable sums of money. What they do

153

contract for is a working partnership with the institution in which both parties have specific roles and responsibilities. These will be defined further on.

Professional fund-raising counsel is usually retained for one or more of the following purposes.

1. *Conducting studies.* The most common fund-raising study is a sophisticated form of market research. Sometimes called a *feasibility study*, it is designed to determine whether, in fact, the institution's specific long- and/or short-term development goals can be achieved.

2. *Providing campaign management.* Once it has been decided to conduct a campaign, professional counsel may be retained to manage the major portion of the campaign. This service typically includes provision of a full-time resident director and part-time supervision by an officer of the firm.

3. *Consulting.* Frequently in the period prior to (which may also include the study period) or subsequent to a capital campaign, an organization requires professional fund-raising consulting services on a per diem basis. These services may focus on virtually any or every aspect of the institution's development efforts. Consulting is typically provided by an officer of the firm who works with the institution's administration, including the development officer and staff and related volunteers, usually trustees.

The foregoing services are also, of course, provided in various combinations by independent consultants. Let us now look in more detail at the major functions professional counsel performs.

THE STUDY

A study—like market research conducted before a new sales program is launched—is almost always an essential prelude to a successful capital campaign. Its purpose is to determine accurately an organization's capital fund-raising potential or, to put it another way, to test in the marketplace the "case" for the institution, the level and commitment of available or potential leadership, and the willingness of prospects to lend the requisite levels of support.

Although exceptions to the rule probably exist, it is axiomatic that an institution cannot conduct a feasibility study for itself by itself. The probability of distorting (however unintentionally) or misinterpreting data, and of losing credibility with internal and external leadership and donors, is obvious. Furthermore, few if any institutions could expect consistently to obtain the candid, accurate information which is essential to a valid study.

Professional counsel enables the institution to overcome these objections by ensuring objectivity, by bringing long experience in conducting such studies to bear (often including close familiarity with the institution and the area in which it will have to seek support), and, perhaps most important of all, by guaranteeing the confidentiality of all information gathered during the study. Consequently, key individuals within the institution and on the outside will consent to be interviewed and speak frankly.

The study report presents a summary of the study findings in which individual respondents are not identified by name. (Nor is the institution shown or given access to counsel's confidential interview reports.) As a result, professionally conducted feasibility studies can assemble the data necessary to forecast with impressive accuracy an institution's potential for meeting its specific capital and other fund-raising objectives.

Sometimes, of course, the findings of a study are negative, indicating that the institution cannot raise the funds it seeks, or raise them in the envisioned time frame. Such findings are not always accepted by the institution's board and administration; nor, indeed, are positive study outcomes always immediately acted upon. A host of variables are obviously involved in each instance. But, interestingly, *very rarely* are the objectivity and the accuracy of professionally conducted feasibility studies brought into question.

Whether the recommendations of a study report are acted upon at once, eventually, or never, as a consequence of the study process an institution typically gains a much clearer view of its strengths and weaknesses, with respect to its fund-raising capability as well as to the ways it is perceived by its internal and external constituencies, and of the strengths or weaknesses of those constituencies. When a feasibility study indicates that more preparation is needed before a successful campaign effort can be initiated, the institution is in a better position to assess its resources for this task and judge what outside assistance will be required. Similarly, the experience of working with professional counsel during the study helps the board and administration better understand the role counsel can and usually should play in the institution's development planning and management efforts, including a capital campaign.

There is usually no contractual or other obligation for an institution to employ the same fund-raising firm which conducted a feasibility study to manage an ensuing capital campaign. It sometimes happens, indeed, for a variety of reasons that the decision is made to use a different firm, although there is no doubt that a well-conducted study can result in laying the groundwork for the working partnership between institution and counsel that is essential for a successful capital effort. Particularly with reference to the important question of personal compatibility—"chemistry," if you will—the study experience helps the organization and counsel alike to evaluate the ability of the personalities involved to work together productively and smoothly. Study costs are almost always computed on a fee or project basis, according to the number of interviews and/or amount of counsel's time required. Expenses for travel, lodging, and so forth are usually billed separately.

CAMPAIGN MANAGEMENT

The study establishes the pattern for the institution and professional counsel in the management and operation of the capital campaign. The point of departure is the study report conclusions and recommendations. In some cases, the pre-campaign study process may be combined with efforts essential to the campaign itself, such as enlistment of campaign leadership and identification of major gifts. Obviously, this can be done only in cases where the feasibility of the campaign has already been determined and the emphasis of the study is on corroborating this and, more particularly, identifying specific leadership and support sources.

The entire campaign scenario must be plotted carefully and realistically against the backdrop of information resulting from the study process. Counsel's study report normally suggests specific campaign dollar and time goals, budgets, and the roles of the trustees, the administration, other parts of the institutional "family," and, finally, professional counsel in the campaign. Reexamination and reconfirmation of these recommendations, then, become the first part of counsel's role in the campaign. A program director (sometimes called the resident or campaign director), chosen for the particular suitability of his experience and his compatibility with the key individuals he will be working with at the institution, is assigned. Counsel also usually assigns a senior officer of the firm as part-time supervisor and indicates which ancillary and support services (described more fully in a later section) it can best furnish.

As in the study, a professional fund-raising firm brings an outside, objective point of view to bear on campaign management. It should be emphasized that professional counsel's role is *not* to relieve the institution's board and administration of their responsibilities for the success of the campaign—for the simple reason that *no* campaign can succeed without their active and sustained involvement. (This important point is amplified in Chapter 2.) Indeed, it must be understood by the institution that once professional campaign management gets under way, key institutional leadership is going to have to work harder than ever! The commitment to the campaign and its goals, enthusiastically pledged at board meetings, must now be matched by commensurate willingness to follow through (and this does not mean only writing a check for a leadership gift, although that too, of course, is essential).

One example may perhaps illustrate the primacy of the role of the institution's top leadership throughout a capital campaign. As made clear in earlier chapters, counsel will virtually never solicit gifts directly. Counsel *will* know all about gifts and their pace-setting role and make recommendations accordingly. These recommendations should be heeded, for—to pursue this particular example—too much haste in seeking to wrap up leadership gifts (a natural tendency) will almost always result in such gifts being accepted at too low a level. Counsel will know, based on the information elicited in the prospect-rating process (see Chapter 5, "Procedures"), what levels are acceptable for various prospect categories.

But, to return to the main point here, the institution's board, administration, and key volunteers will have to do the actual asking, which will require time. In addition to personal solicitations, there will be foundation presentations, social and other functions, various and frequently numerous (but important) campaign-related meetings, work with volunteers, and so forth, which, as essential ingredients of the campaign master plan, can *only* be implemented successfully with the full cooperation and involvement of the trustees and other top campaign leadership.

The point is stressed because experience shows that these individuals, as eager as they are to assist the institution, often underestimate the amount of actual time—during the working day, during evenings, on weekends—which goes into a successful capital campaign. Hence an important function of professional counsel in campaign management is to provide frequent, accurate feedback to key institutional leadership about the progress of the campaign, special needs and problems which may develop, and so forth. Effective counsel will never hesitate to let the institution or volunteer leadership know when additional attention or effort is needed.

It is important, and probably comforting, to bear in mind that in the management of a capital campaign, counsel, like the institution, has a great deal at stake—no less indeed than its professional reputation. Hence it can be taken for granted that reputable counsel will discharge responsibilities in every area at the highest level of professionalism. While regrettable lapses do infrequently occur, the number of professional firms which have maintained outstanding reputations for quality and probity for over half a century (the "lifetime" of the profession) testifies to the industry's adherence to the highest professional and ethical standards.

Campaign management is normally provided on a fee basis for a specified time period, which may be abridged or terminated, usually on 60 or so days' notice, by the client institution or the consulting firm.

CONSULTING

Professional consulting by a senior officer of a fund-raising firm is normally provided on a per diem basis. Often, the goal of such consulting arrangements is to assist an organization to prepare internally for a heightened development effort, usually with the recognition that a capital campaign will become necessary but cannot be contemplated until the board, administration, volunteer leadership, and other groups such as faculty, medical staff, alumni, or the like have been better prepared. Professional counsel may also be employed for consultation on specific aspects of an institution's development and fund-raising efforts, including annual giving, deferred giving, public relations and communications, recruitment, and so on.

AUXILIARY SERVICES

Professional fund-raising firms usually provide a variety of ancillary support services requiring close integration with the campaign effort. The advantages, in most instances, of contracting for these services as a part of overall campaign management are obvious. The services typically include writing (case statements, campaign publications, proposals and special presentations, speeches), public relations, direct-mail and computer applications, prospect research, and so forth. Certain campaign management services, such as guidance in setting up a campaign office, prospect files, and gift acknowledgments, are also sometimes provided separately by counsel when an institution requires assistance only in one of these specific areas. Charges for ancillary services are usually made either on a per diem or project basis. Cost estimates for these services are generally included in the overall proposed budget for campaign management.

Independent Consultants and Free-Lancers

Numerous individuals offer their services as independent or free-lance fund-raising consultants. Quality and experience vary far more widely than among established, reputable firms, but obviously, skilled and experienced independent consultants are available, if not in any great number. The chief reason is probably that with the exception of a few highly respected senior consultants, it is much more difficult for an individual effectively to assist a broad range of not-for-profit institutions than it is for a professional firm which can offer more services in greater depth, for an equivalent expenditure.

Nevertheless, professionally established and qualified independent consultants can play an important role by providing specific consulting services in specialized areas, by offering small or nascent institutions access to limited professional fund-raising services which a firm could not economically supply, and by serving institutions in regions where, for various reasons, professional firms are not active. The biggest difficulty, from the institution's standpoint, in deciding to use independents is the question of choice, which also applies, in somewhat different ways, to professional firms.

Selecting Professional Counsel

Selecting the professional fund-raising firm or independent consultant best suited to a particular institution and its needs at a given time is probably as taxing and perplexing as choosing one's spouse, and certainly more difficult than, say, deciding on a personal physician. The reason is the heady mixture of subjective and objective factors which come into consideration simultaneously, and the lack of widespread accreditation standards. In the case of independent consultants and "free-lancers," there are virtually *no* accreditation criteria at the present time.

While any individual can hang out his shingle as a "professional fund-raising consultant," it is obvious that organizing and sustaining a professional firm requires qualities which *may* be present in the "independent" but are not requisite to his survival, at least for the short term. These qualities are well stated in the American Association of Fund-Raising Counsel's fair practice code:

1. Member firms will serve only those nonprofit institutions or agencies whose purpose and methods they can approve. They will not knowingly be used by any organization to induce philanthropically inclined persons to give their money to unworthy causes.

2. Member firms do business only on the basis of a specified fee, determined prior to the beginning of the campaign. They will not serve clients on the unprofessional basis of a percentage or commission of the sums raised. They maintain this ethical standard also by not profiting, directly or indirectly, from disbursements for the accounts of clients.

3. The executive head of a member organization must demonstrate at least a six-year record of continuous experience as a professional in the fund-raising field. This helps to protect the public from those who enter the profession without sufficient competence, experience, or devotion to ideals of public service.

4. The Association looks with disfavor upon firms which use methods harmful to the public, such as making exaggerated claims of past achievements, guaranteeing results, and promising to raise unobtainable sums.

5. No payment in cash or kind shall be made by a member to an officer, director, trustee, or adviser of a philanthropic agency or institution as compensation for using his influence for the engaging of a member for fund-raising counsel.

The AAFRC's membership, of course, includes most of the major fund-raising firms active today, including many of those—mostly in the East—which have been around long enough to establish solid track records. And a firm's track record, or professional reputation, is probably the single most important criterion in choosing counsel. (It goes without saying that there are professional fund-raising firms which are *not* AAFRC members but which adhere to the same basic fair practice tenets.)

Institutions should of course be aware that membership in a recognized professional association does not constitute a guarantee of anything. While the AAFRC member firms, for example, subscribe fully to its fair practice code, other worthy professional associations such as the National Society of Fund Raising Executives (NSFRE) and the National Association for Hospital Development (NAHD) list in their directories as "consultants" all who wish their names to appear. Such listings, sometimes superficially similar to the AAFRC membership list, for example, are basically different in the sense that they do not reflect subscription by those listed to a stated code of professional ethics or practice.

Other organizations too maintain lists of fund-raising counsel—the National Health Council, the National Information Bureau, the Philanthropic Advisory Service to the Better Business Bureau, and so forth. The essential distinction to be made is between membership in, or listings in the directories of, a professional association with established, publicly stated codes of practice and associations which simply print the names of practicing professionals. The basic need underscored by this situation, from the standpoint of institutions selecting professional fund-raising counsel, is for standarized accreditation and uniform certification standards. It is probable that the fund-raising industry will move more decisively in this direction in the coming decade.

Meanwhile, the ultimate criterion, probably at once the most decisive and potentially most confusing, remains the firm's or individual's track record or professional reputation. This can be tested by inquiring among former clients of the firms or individuals under consideration. How would the institution evaluate their services? Were cost estimates reasonably accurate? Were the organization's objectives in hiring counsel met? Would the institution engage the same firm or individual again for a similar program?

Obviously, sound business practice dictates checking with *several* of each prospective firm's or individual's former clients. The greatest disadvantage of the referral or word-of-mouth approach to selecting counsel is its potential for creating confusion. Inevitably, individual perceptions differ; professional counsel achieves greater perceived and/or measured effectiveness under one set of circumstances than another; and subjective judgments are fallible. Nevertheless, the writer knows of no better or more reliable way, particularly in the case of "unaccredited" firms and independents, than running a careful, thorough check on the track record of each organization or individual under consideration. The time required for this will be amply rewarded if it results in the choice of professional fund-raising counsel meeting the five criteria cited above and able to work effectively with a particular institution and its board and administrative leadership.

Some Maxims
and Rules of Thumb

Every profession generates a collection of axioms, formulas, maxims, prescriptions, and what might be called rules of thumb, which reflect the accumulated experience of its practitioners. While these axioms are perhaps seldom "profound," they frequently convey significant ideas in pithy and sometimes even memorable form. The following list, which does not claim to be encyclopedic, presents some of the more applicable fund-raising maxims encountered during forty years' professional fund-raising experience.

PHILANTHROPY

Voluntary, eleemosynary organizations are found *only* in democracies. Their extent and health are certain barometers of democratic values. They are invariably among the first victims of totalitarianism—because no coercive system can foster true volunteerism.

Always remember there is no "ceiling" on philanthropy. Individuals can give as much as they want; and corporations can give nearly *five times* as much as they have been giving for the past decade. In short: keep asking, keep raising sights, keep the "heat" on—because the money's there.

FUND RAISING IN GENERAL

The rule of the fives: The most effective solicitation structure (for control) is one "captain" to each five committee members and one solicitor to every five prospects.

Solicitations are most effective at the peer level or down.

Sequential fund raising works from the inside out and the top down.

You can't fish when the fly is in the boat, and you can't raise money without asking for it. Like milking a cow, you've got to sit right down and go to work.

Giving sights are raised dramatically by pledges (payable over three to five years) in a capital campaign, and by monthly payroll deductions in an annual campaign.

The response of the prospective donor will be in direct proportion to the commitment and enthusiasm of the solicitor.

Having given himself, he who asks with confidence gets far better results.

When seeking substantial capital funds from philanthropic sources, it is wise to start on the premise that you are first looking for one donor who can give it all. Failing that, you next look for the total amount from two givers. Failing that, look for three, and so on. The point is, always pay the greatest attention to the greatest potential.

Don't assume that a goal cannot be reached because it has never been reached (or attempted) before—that is fatal!

Publicity doesn't raise money; someone has to do the asking.

"I'm a lousy fund raiser" fairly often translates into "I'm a lousy giver."

Know your prospect. Many an institution has suffered remorse because "we didn't know he could give that kind of money."

The person who "hates fund raising" most likely has been asked to take on a job he or she just isn't adequately trained for.

Get over the idea that you have to apologize for asking! If your cause is deserving, it doesn't ever have to be apologized for. If your cause is not deserving, don't apologize—don't even ask!

Most often you will get better results from soliciting those who are *not* your friends.

"Nice guys" are tempted to accept small gifts. Don't settle for less than what's right!

Persist, but with sensitivity. You will be respected!

Success on the battlefield begins in the camp. Devote the necessary time to getting ready. Plan your strategy. Avoid heroics. Be deliberate.

Nothing substitutes for face-to-face solicitation. The higher the giving potential, the wider the spread between results from personal solicitation and any other form of asking. For example: a personal call will produce $50 to every $10 produced by telephone and to every $1 produced by direct mail. Never forget these ratios when someone says "I'll phone him" or "I'll write." Go and *see* him whenever possible!

Report all gifts quickly; the big ones will help raise the sights of other donors.

Cultivation—in the fund-raising sense—is not personal ingratiation. It is the heightening of interest in the cause at hand—in other words, education.

In all but exceptional cases, leadership-gift solicitation is accomplished most effectively by a team of two or three solicitors. The reasons: (1) there is strength in numbers, and a team can be mutually supportive in a task many find difficult; (2) the prospect will be flattered; (3) a team is more likely to cover all the sales points effectively and less likely to accept a refusal or token gift.

In talking with prospects, *always* begin by suggesting a contribution at the upper limit of their considered giving ability. If you are high, the prospect will not take offense—gifts, like water, will eventually find their own level.

Remember, campaigns fail because prospects are not seen, not because they refuse to give!

OBTAINING PLEDGES

Whenever possible, get the donor to complete and sign the institution's pledge card. It is usually legally binding on the donor, his heirs, or estate. Do *not* leave the pledge card with the prospect; all too often, this results in a pledge for an inadequate amount. Be prepared to make several calls on your prospect to get the pledge you want, on a pledge card.

When a donor cannot or will not make a gift by means of the pledge card, obtain a letter of intent. Remember, it is essential that pledges be formalized in writing. Verbal pledges should be accepted only as a last resort—and counted when paid.

It is human to find some fault even with what we love most. Always allow room for the prospect's point of view and minor criticisms of the cause you are asking him to support. Remember the old saying: If you want to persuade someone, you cannot afford to be more than 85 percent correct.

Every worthwhile organization and cause can present a compelling case—if the job is done right. One element that has no place in an effective statement of the case is the suggestion that prospects "owe" the institution something because it rendered services at less than cost. This will simply strike many as poor management. Emphasize instead the differences the services rendered have made, and their importance for the future.

DIRECT MAIL

Use the eye-to-eye, belly-to-belly approach in solicitation letter copy, writing as you would speak in person. It works!

DEFERRED GIVING

An individual who has the means and probably would be willing to support an institution, and who is never asked, almost always *will* take it with him, as far as that institution is concerned.

First, get the cash gift, then the pledge (hopefully with fast payment), then the deferred gift (insurance, annuity, unitrusts), and last, the bequest.

CAPITAL CAMPAIGNS

A successful capital campaign increases the level of annual giving in subsequent years, as the rising tide raises all the boats.

Index